D1230689

Welcome to Greatness

A Wakeup Call for Your Journey En Route to Fulfillment

Alex Nosa Ihama

BALBOA PRESS
A DIVISION OF HAY HOUSE

ISBN: 978-1-4525-3685-9 (sc)
ISBN: 978-1-4525-3684-2 (e)
ISBN: 978-1-4525-3686-6 (hc)

Library of Congress Control Number: 2011912041

Balboa Press books may be ordered through booksellers or by contacting:

Balboa Press
A Division of Hay House
1663 Liberty Drive
Bloomington, IN 47403
www.balboapress.com
1-(877) 407-4847

Printed in the United States of America
Balboa Press rev. date: 03/30/2012

To everyone who has accompanied me thus far
as a coach or a client in my personal journey en route to fulfillment.
Thank you for graciously taking the time to coach me,
for honourably allowing me to coach you.
Thank you.

Contents

Preface

Everything we do or say is a conscious or subconscious attempt to derive some form of satisfaction in life, whether we know it or not. We say and do things to appease our ego and then tell ourselves that it is for the benefit of others. We pursue a selfish objective and then tell ourselves that it will position us to assist other people. We chase after money, power and fame and then tell ourselves that we will expend it all for the betterment of the world. I lived like this for many years until some series of unfortunate events forced me to begin my journey en route to fulfillment, until recurring challenges forced me to begin a revolutionary change in mindset, which eventually empowered me to overcome detrimental character traits that were holding me back from welcoming greatness into my life.

We live in a world where many of us are so blindly driven that we have become oblivious to the obvious fact that the people who eventually attained whatever it is we are now pursing did not end up attaining the fulfillment we are expecting to attain. We have heard of the saying that money does not buy happiness, but yet we continue to spend our lives pursuing money with the subconscious hope of buying happiness with it. In fact, some people would nod agreeably at the revolutionary principles and strategies that this book has to offer, but yet will continue to live lives that are not reflective of the principles and strategies they so strongly agree with.

When I decided to change my life for the better over a decade ago, little did I know it was a lifelong journey and not the one-time event that most of us often think it to be. I discovered that those detrimental character traits that took me a long time to develop required an even longer time to break. I discovered that the more changes I made in my character, the more changes I still needed to make. It seems like every change I made exposed other flaws in my character that required more changes.

I discovered that we cannot say, "I am now a better leader and thus no longer need to work on my leadership capabilities". We cannot say, "I am now very generous and thus no longer need to work at being generous anymore". Without a question, the process of change is a lifelong journey, and this book is a roadmap of the tedious journey based on my personal experience and the experiences of a number of people who I have been fortunate enough to coach and speak to in my line of work.

After successfully overcoming many deterrents of fulfillment in my own life and after having successfully coached thousands of people through different mediums on how to overcome their deterrents of fulfillment as well, I now realize that the art of changing one's life for the better requires an unwavering daily commitment to a set of principles that have stood the test of time. This book is a humble attempt to empower and equip you with those principles based on my personal experiences and that of the people who have graciously allowed me to work and walk with them in their individual journey en route to fulfillment.

My prayer and hope is not only for you to learn new things from this book, but also for you to unlearn the detrimental habits, baseless concepts, and diluted perspectives that you may have picked up in your childhood or along the highway of life. It is for you to recognize how steeped you may be in a cocktail of fear, procrastination, insecurity, laziness, greed, selfishness, hate, pride, arrogance and whatever it is that may be holding you back from welcoming greatness into your life. My prayer and hope for those of you who are enthusiastic about discovering the beauty within you is for the Almighty God to open your eyes to the unseen even when you are in doubt, replenish your strength even before it depletes, and direct your step even before you take it. My prayer and hope is for you to learn how to purify your character and relax your soul.

The principles that you will be exposed to in this book, I have made every effort to foster–and will continually do so until death relieves me of my purpose in life. These principles are based on years of deep psychological, physiological, spiritual and philosophical researches which transcend religious, cultural, racial and socio-economic backgrounds. Those who have been acquainted with these principles through our coaching programs, speaking engagements, life researches and publications continue to bless us with their words of encouragement. They continue to share with us the impact they are now making in the world based on these principles. These principles have helped many people to attain peace of mind despite growing adversity, stronger opposition, consistent oppression and never-ending life and business challenges.

As you embark on your journey en route to fulfillment, which is the most fulfilling journey in life according to those who have being on this road less travelled, open the doors of your heart and narrow the entrance to your soul. Fasten your seat belt ahead of the revolutionary changes that stubbornly lie ahead of you. In addition, be prepared to be challenged by yourself and by others, to be compelled by your body and your soul. Be prepared to meet yourself, to get acquainted with the real you; to motivate yourself and to lead yourself through whatever it may take to stay this daunting course.

Since I began my journey en route to fulfillment over a decade ago, I have come to enormously appreciate people like you who are seeking to be better, people who are making every effort to not depart this world without having made an impact on it. My transformation from darkness to light and from living for self to living for others was made possible by the Grace of God through a number of people, some of whom I knew personally and sought help and advice from, and others whom I may never meet personally but yet was equipped by how they lived their lives.

I have learnt that fulfillment is not a destination but rather a journey. It begins at every wake and does not end until we return to dust. The time to begin the journey en route to fulfillment is now, for later is a thief of time, a major hindrance to the fulfillment that we seek in life. Until we learn to not procrastinate, to not put aside what has already been put aside once, to not give in to excuses for not beginning the journey that we must embark on, the fulfillment we claim to desire will elude us.

I have learnt that life is not about how rich and talented we are, but rather about how often we bless others with what we have, with who we are, with what we know. Life is about using our wisdom, talents and resources to empower other people so that they may be equipped enough to conquer their own challenges, blaze their own trails and impact their own spheres. Until we are open, every door of opportunity will be closed. Until we are learning, we will never be able to grow and achieve. Until we are giving, we will always be in want. It is only when all hands are on deck that the ship has a better chance of arriving safely at its destination. Until then, the fate of the ship is in the hands of chance that does not exist.

As you take control of yourself and embark on the journey of your life, I wish you bon voyage. May God disperse his most powerful angels to protect you every step of the way in your honourable journey en route to fulfillment. May you not be distracted, disconcerted or discouraged. May every effort you make be blessed by God and may your new way of being inspire those around you to even greater heights.

Nothing but love!

Introduction

While most people often wait to hit rock bottom like I did before embarking on their individual journey en route to fulfillment, it does not have to be so for you. While most people often wait to learn the hard way, you do not have to experience the pains and challenges of debts, divorce, desperation, dejection, disillusion, discouragement and depression like I did before you embark on your journey en route to fulfillment. If we only knew just a little bit more about ourselves and about life itself, we would be able to mitigate most of the pains and challenges that we are experiencing or, at least, manage them effectively as they come. Welcome to Greatness was written to empower and equip you to break through your present challenges to a future of fulfillment.

Unlike physical journeys which have starting and ending points, mental, emotional or spiritual journeys only have beginnings, for they end when we end. If we wish to attain the fulfillment that we claim to desire, then the journey will become our life, and our life, the journey. Without a question, the process of character changes and human development is a lifelong journey, and this book is a roadmap of the journey based on my personal experience and the experiences of a number of people who are on the same journey as well. It is an account of what the journey en route to fulfillment looks like–what it takes to start it, what to expect en route, and what is involved to sustain it.

The type of greatness referred to in this book is not the shallow definition that measures people based on fame, riches and power, but rather on love, humility and servitude. The type of greatness that is referred to in this book has nothing to do with riches, but rather how you acquired it and what you do with it. It has nothing to do with fame but rather how you acquired it and how you are managing it. It has nothing to do with power, but rather how you acquired it and how you are using it to make the world a better place. You can be very rich, famous and powerful and still be great in love, humility and servitude; and this book is a roadmap of how to make it happen.

Welcome to Greatness is an account of a very personal journey from a life of absolute self to that of absolute best; from a life of regrettable disservice to humanity to that of a passionate service for mankind. The journey is broken down into three phases: Self-Discovery, Self-Awareness and Self-Actualization, for to ensure our safe arrival at a desired destination, it is critical to know who we are (Self-Discovery), where we are (Self-Awareness), and how to get there (Self-Actualization). We cannot expect to arrive at wherever we set out to go without first knowing who we are, where we are, and how we are going to get there. It is also important to know why we are embarking on the journey in the first place. I decided to embark on my journey en route to fulfillment in order to avoid self-destruction, for I had ignored the divine calling within me for too long that it was causing me to loose enormous amount of sleep every night, and making me live a life of suspicion; suspicion of myself and everyone else.

The Self-Discovery Phase is about knowing who you are, and why you think, speak and act the way you do. It is about knowing why some pains and challenges seem to recur in your life, and how to develop the confidence that is required for this lifelong journey. This is also the phase where you discover your purpose in life and identify whatever is required for you to safely arrive at your destination. It is about getting acquainted with your detrimental character traits as well as your beneficial ones, and about knowing how you may leverage them for the betterment of mankind.

The act of Self-Discovery is mentally strenuous and emotionally draining because it requires us to recall the pains and challenges that we went through in the past, especially those abusive ones that tend to leave lasting impact on us. This is a critical step in the journey en route to fulfillment–to understand what may have happened at inception to make us form some of the character traits that are now deterrents of fulfillment in our lives.

The four chapters in the Self-Discovery Phase are sequenced in a way to ease the challenges that are expected in this elementary stage of your journey. To maximize your experience, you may need to engage in therapy if compelled. Just as it is unwise to take your vehicle on the longest journey in your lifetime without first having performed a thorough check-up, it is unwise to begin the journey en route to fulfillment without first having discovered yourself. Regardless of whatever you are engaged in, you will be as fulfilled in life as what you know about yourself, life itself, and the world you live in.

This first phase in the journey en route to fulfillment is an attempt to make it easy for you to face yourself, identify your deterrents of fulfillment, and build the courage that is required for you to embark on your journey. Approach it with an open mind and a strong willingness to break through any hindrance and you will greatly benefit from it. Even though most of us would rather downplay or deny the abuse we went through as children, bringing it to light and accepting it is very necessary for healing.

The Self-Awareness Phase is about being aware of your character traits; your strengths and weaknesses. It is about being aware of how what you think, say and do either instigates or inhibits progress in your journey en route to fulfillment. Self-awareness is a perpetual state of being for those who are willing to sustain their journey en route to fulfillment. When we stop being self-aware, we would gradually fall behind in our journey and eventually go back to our old ways of being.

This is the phase where you get to equip yourself with proven strategies of fulfillment in life, where you get to know more about yourself in order to maintain a forward momentum in your journey. There are many things to be aware of in life, but the five chapters in this phase are amongst the most critical things to be self-aware of. Just as it is wise to be aware of the roadblocks en route your physical journey, so is it wise to be aware of things that may be deterring the progress of your mental, emotional and spiritual journey. So is it wise to be self-aware at all times.

The Self-Actualization Phase is about following through on the outcomes of your Self-Discovery and Self-Awareness Phases. It is about taking the necessary action to sustain your journey en route to fulfillment. This is where you get to make things happen, where you get to align your actions with your new way of being. By the time you reach this phase, your purpose in life must be clear; the focus and discipline that you require to sustain your journey must be sharpened; and your destination must be obvious to you and everyone else around you.

While it is often considered by many as the height of human existence, self-actualization is not the end of the journey en route to fulfillment, but rather the beginning of a new phase. As you will find in the five chapters in this phase, our journey en route to fulfillment is not only about making things happen for ourselves, but also about making things happen for those around us. This is why we must continue our journey from self-actualization to self-fulfillment. Like the final leg in an iron man race, it is only the strong and determined that often gets this far in the journey en route to fulfilment; it is only the prayerful and humble that will survive it.

As you read through the book, it is wise to periodically reflect on your progress so that you may tighten any loose end along the way. Reflect on the phrases and principles that resonates with you and write down what you intend to remember. Maintain the urgency that is required to sustain the journey, without rushing through it. If there was any time that focus on self is not being selfish, it is in the process of learning. Welcome to Greatness is all about focus on self-growth; what you need to do in order to become the change you desire in the world, in order to live life to the fullest, in order to welcome greatness into your life.

This is my story; a story that is similar to that of millions of people around the world. An account of how the minds of many of us were intentionally or unintentionally shifted from its natural state of love to the superficial states of fear, guilt, hate, greed, selfishness, nonchalance, ignorance, arrogance and insecurity. Welcome to Greatness is not just a book for your reading pleasure, but most importantly, written to introduce you to yourself and equip you with the skills, principles and strategies which are necessary to sustain your personal growth.

It was written to expose you to the abounding strength, overwhelming intelligence and striking beauty that you likely never even knew existed within you. It was written to compel you to face yourself and whomever or whatever you need to face in order to begin living your life to the fullest. A lot of effort was put into it to ensure it appeals to you from psychological, physiological, spiritual and philosophical standpoints, while exhorting and encouraging you to the pinnacle of your existence. It will require a lot of effort from you to come out of yourself and get out of your way to achieve greatness.

Full of wisdom from real life experiences and proven strategies of success in key areas of life, Welcome to Greatness is captivating, challenging and compelling. The passionate urgency in which this personal journey en route to fulfillment is told will provoke your thoughts, ravish your heart and stir your soul. It is bound to make you think deeply, act passionately and grow steadily.

Bon voyage!

Phase 1:

Self-Discovery

> The greatest explorer on this earth never takes voyages as long as those of the man who descends to the depth of his heart.
>
> ~Julien Green

Chapter 1

Inception

> **"The greatest revolution of our generation is the discovery that human beings, by changing the inner attitudes of their minds, can change the outer aspects of their lives."**
>
> **~ Williams James**

Everything has a beginning, including our mindset. How we think, see, hear, feel and talk is a combination of our upbringing, genetics, environment, and our level of exposure, education and experience. Chief amongst these are our upbringing and childhood experiences, for these are the most instrumental aspects in the shaping of our mindsets. Inception is a tale of the beginning, a journey back into the past to better understand the present and clearly see the future. As we begin our journey en route to fulfillment, it is absolutely crucial to understand why we think, see, hear, feel and talk the way we do. It is this understanding that will enable us to identify why we are where we are in every aspect of our lives.

As soon as I was able to grasp it, I thought about it, said it, watched it or did it. Be it vulgarism of all sorts, theft of anything that may not have even been worth the while, or promiscuity with those who were weak-willed like I was, I engaged in many self-gratifying and despicable act at the expense of other people in order to nurture my ego. With a very strong focus on myself, and myself only, I cared less about what the right thing to do was and more about what I wanted to do. Even though people were consistently bruised by my aggressive attempts to get what I wanted and constantly injured by my neediness to be praised, I thought I was not that bad as long as no one else's life was literally at stake.

I was so full of myself and so steeped in my atrocities that the cries of my conscience were numbed by my nonchalance to the pain I caused other people, by my arrogance in every situation, and by my ignorance about what really mattered most in life. I pursued money and material possessions fervently; what I wanted, I got at all costs. Despite having attended church regularly until my teenage years, I cared less about godly principles and societal laws. I did not hesitate to walk over anybody in my attempt to satisfy my insatiable desires, in my efforts to nurture my tumultuous ego.

Looking back in my life prior to the beginning of my journey en route to fulfillment, and looking around me today, any one would wonder what happened to some of us in our childhood to make us become so hardened at heart, so fearful and so insecure; to make us become completely deaf to the cries of our consciences and so selfishly focused on ourselves to the extent that those around us are consistently bruised by our nonchalance, arrogance, ignorance. How did we gradually get transformed from human beings that were created in the image and likeness of God to pitiable creatures that live in such obvious contradiction to the image and likeness of God who created us?

How did I gradually get transformed from a church boy to a fraudster, from a kid who everyone loved to a youth who the law despised, from a teenager who was made to skip a high school grade due to higher level of intelligence to a university dropout? How could I have completely disregarded the godly values that were imbibed in me as a child to become a pitiable person that the world longed to do without? How could I have walked myself into the bottomless pit that I found myself over a decade ago prior to summoning the courage to embark on my personal journey en route to fulfillment?

You may have also looked around you and wondered how loving people gradually become haters of many; how action-oriented people gradually become irritating whiners; how kind people suddenly become so wicked, and how family-oriented people selfishly give up their families for promiscuity, drugs and parties. Years into my journey, I realized that while most of us may be shocked by where we find ourselves in life, we have been heading in that direction all the while. Where you are today, right here, right now–whether in your personality, leadership, marriage, parenting, spirituality, relationships, health and wellness, academics, career, finances and business–is a direct result of your psychological makeup; the way you think, the choices you made, the mindset you foster. Someone else may have created an unfortunate path for you to follow as a child, but you led yourself to where you are today as an adult.

Regardless of whatever transpired in our upbringing to create fear, hate, doubt, greed and selfishness in us, there is still love in abundance within us. We may have been programmed by incapable parents to only think of ourselves, the urge to love and serve one another remains alive within us. Nothing that was done to us can extinguish the innate desire to overcome the past and aim for a fulfilling future. The fact that many refuse to begin their journey en route to fulfillment does not mean that they are not being reminded by their consciences every now and then. I was.

In my journey en route to fulfillment, I have learnt that until we begin to claim full responsibility for our decisions and actions, and even for our reactions to the hurtful behaviours of other people, we will never be at peace. Blaming our unfortunate situations and negative feelings on other people and basing our action and inaction on whether other people fulfill their responsibilities or not are the immature attitudes that separate children from adults. We are where we are in life today because we walked ourselves there, because we neither paid attention to the warning signs along the highway of life nor humbly accepted the advice which we were graciously offered by those who cared, those who may have even put their friendship on the line to wake us up from our spiritual slumber. We do not fall into trouble; we often see it ahead of us and yet walk right into it anyway, and then claim to have fallen into it.

In my journey en route to fulfillment, I have learnt that the most ferocious battles to have ever been fought were neither of the two world wars nor the wars that ravished Vietnam, Afghanistan and Iraq. While the world will forever be scarred by these atrocities of men, the greatest battles in life are those we fight in our minds every day; the battles of love versus hate, good versus evil, forgiveness versus revenge, selflessness versus selfishness, humility versus vanity. I have learnt that the true success of a man lies not necessarily in the works of his hands, but rather in his ability to consistently control his mind, soften his heart, and connect with his spirit. These are what determine the durability of his work, the sustainability of his journey.

Until we learn to control our mind, we will never be able to control our words or our actions. Until we learn to win against the negative thoughts that we struggle with everyday, some of these thoughts will eventually manifest themselves into unimaginable scales of human catastrophe. The worst atrocities the world has ever seen, like slavery, the holocaust, and the ethnic cleansings which resulted in the gruesome killing of over two million people in Yugoslavia and Rwanda were initially thoughts in the minds of the perpetrators until those thoughts, after being nurtured for a while, were maliciously transformed into series of very unfortunate events in the history of mankind. Without a doubt, whatever we carry in your mind today, whether good or bad, intentional or unintentional, will eventually carry us along tomorrow.

It is unfortunate that some parents exposed their children to so much domestic violence, that some parents were not examples of love, integrity and spirituality to their children. It is unfortunate that some people have allowed their detrimental life experiences to hinder the love they must give to others, that some societies are not doing enough to deter the wicked from influencing others in the wrong direction. It is unfortunate that some of us do not feel protected enough by our governments, organizations, friends and families. But the inconvenient truth is that we are still and will always be 100% responsible for our actions, 100% responsible for the experiences that we choose to welcome into our lives. Some one may have hurt us very bad, but it is us who choose to remain hurt.

In the 2010 blockbuster movie, Inception, the main character, played by Leonardo DiCaprio, was a specialized spy and corporate espionage thief. While his work consisted of secretly extracting valuable commercial information from the unconscious mind of his targets when they were asleep and dreaming, the movie was mainly about him trying to infiltrate the mind of a target and plant an idea in his mind without the target's knowledge. More like a mind game, this idea, when implanted in the mind of this target, is meant to get him to make certain decisions that he would certainly regret afterwards. This is what transpired in the lives of many of us when we were growing up. Some of the ideas that were knowingly or unknowingly implanted in our minds during our upbringing are not beneficial to us; in fact, some of these ideas may even be dangerous and self-destructive. Telling children to not say hello to strangers is a very common one, while another one is warning children to stay away from a particular ethnic group because of a biased preconceived notion of that particular ethnic group.

The minds of many people in today's societies are adulterated because their parents did not do enough to protect them from the pollution of the world, from the decadence of nowadays. This is why many people think, say or do the things that they eventually regret. This is why the workaholic, who knows that the proof of love is the investment of time, still spends all his time at work to the detriment of his family, and then wonders why his wife left him and why his children are wayward. This is why the fraudulent, the adulterous, the thieves, the liars, the rapists and murderers, who know they are breaking godly and societal laws, continue to do so anyway.

These people think, say or do things against their own consciences either because they no longer have control of their minds or because they have completely lost their minds altogether. In the words of St. Augustine, "People travel to wonder at the height of mountains, at the huge waves of the sea, at the long courses of rivers, at the vast compass of the ocean, at the circular motion of the stars; and they pass by themselves without wondering." Like me during my days of rebellion, their minds were adulterated during their childhood and are now being influenced by their detrimental childhood experiences rather than by the influence of God whom they claim to believe in.

It is not often what we were told to do or not to do as a child that got our minds twisted, but rather what we saw, what we heard and what we experienced. A parent may not have directly warn his child to stay away from a particular ethnic group; however, if he stays away from that particular ethnic group or is often overheard sharing racially prejudiced opinions about the ethnic group, the message of hate is gradually implanted in the child's mind. To the child, that group is bad, and so is everyone who is part of it.

I remember an encounter with a fine young woman right after one of my speaking engagements. She came to me almost in tears, vividly narrating how her uncle had forbidden her about two decades prior from associating with a particular person because he was from a different racial background. She said that she was literally asked to disregard and disrespect that person for so many years that it forced her to stay away from that particular ethnic group altogether. As she began to work through her hatred for this particular ethnic group in her adulthood, that hatred began to transfer itself over to her uncle for having implanted racial prejudice in her at that young age. What an awful experience to subject anyone to, especially children.

In my days of rebellion, the godly principles that I was taught mattered less because I had witnessed so much hypocrisy and experienced so much harshness and hate that protecting and pleasing me at all cost became my utmost priorities. How was I supposed to love my neighbour as myself when those who were meant to be examples of love spoke ill about their neighbours all the time, when some of those who were meant to raise me as a child made me feel hated by how badly they treated me? How was I supposed to have integrity when I was literally taught to lie by adults who believed that staying out of the trouble was more important than upholding integrity?

Because of what many adults saw, heard and experienced in their childhood, they are now remarkably rebellious against reason, obvious nuisances in society and unequivocally disrespectful towards God. They have been hurt so bad during their childhood that all that now matters to them is to please and protect themselves at all cost. They would take very extreme measures to protect themselves from possible hurt, shame, fear, guilt and insecurity, even if it means to ostracize or isolate themselves from everyone else, including their families. Are you in this category? How much control do you really have over your mind? While you are always 100% responsible for your thoughts, words and actions, are you truly 100% in control of your mind, which, apparently controls the thoughts, words and actions that you are 100% responsible for?

It is the difference between our level of responsibility and the amount of control we have over our mind that causes hurt, instigates shame, instils fear, creates guilt and brings about the insecurity that hinders success in every aspect of our life. How can we expect to achieve or sustain anything if we do not have enough control of our mind? To have 100% control of our thoughts, words and actions, we must first have 100% control of our minds. Until then, we will be consistently haunted by the impact of this discrepancy. It is like being responsible for something that we have no control of.

Think about it: Does it make sense to you that you are wary of a particular ethnic group because a few people from it were involved in despicable acts? Does it make sense to you that you choose to no longer donate money to charitable organizations because a few of these organizations were involved in fraudulent activities? Does it make sense to you that you desist from saying hello to strangers in an elevator and even to someone seating right beside you on a six-hour flight because you were told as a child to stay away from strangers? Does it make sense to you that you refuse to go into a church because a few religious leaders were caught in scandalous activities?

Does it make sense to you that you now live a distrustful life because your parents excessively warned you about trusting people? Does it make sense to you that you now live in fear because of a few isolated incidences that may have hurt you in the past? Does it make sense to you that you are now struggling with insecurity because of jests that were made about you ages ago? Does it make sense to you that you are defensive about the detrimental character traits and behaviours that everyone else sees in you?

I have learnt that whatever we always think about will always occur in our lives. If we stick to a certain mindset, we will always act in a certain way. And if we refuse to change our ways, our lives will remain the same. If you are not content with where you are in life today, it is time to change your mindset. If you want different results in your life and leadership, your career and relationships, your business and finances, it is time to change your mindset. It is time to think differently and act passionately so you may grow steadily. Your situation may be unfavourable, but it is your mindset that will determine how long it will last for. Our greatest strength is the ability we have to control our minds, for whether we succeed or fail depends not on what others do or don't do, but rather what we have decided in our minds.

When we start doing what our consciences truly expect of us, doing away with the illusionary reasons that makes us to believe even for just a second that we are not good enough, not smart enough, not strong enough, not talented enough, not charismatic enough and not impacting enough, we would finally come to the awesome realization that the obstacles we consider unnecessary are in fact necessary to prepare us for the challenges that lay ahead of us. Sooner or later, consciously or subconsciously, we will begin to develop the mindset that continues to create heroes out of ordinary people. Until we assume full control of our minds, we will remain captives of other people's imaginations. Until we accept our originality, we will remain other people's inferiority.

Whenever I reminisce about the way I lived before embarking on my journey en route to fulfillment, it is obvious to me that I had lost my mind for many years. In fact, there were definitely times that I thought, spoke and acted as if I did not even have a mind. How else would you explain responding to aggression with aggression, to hate with hate? How else would you explain being vengeful over a hurt that occurred many years prior? How else would you explain living without any form of shame or guilt?

How else would you explain treating people with so much disrespect and wickedness? How else would you explain going through life without a clear purpose? How would you explain living without listening to the conscience, which is the part of human beings that literally makes sense? If you only knew the power of the mind, you would begin to make the necessary effort to get yours back; to protect and gain control over your mind before you either lose it or allow it to lead you into a bottomless pit.

If there was ever a time to take back the control of your mind, it is now. If there was ever a time to desire revolutionary changes in your life and society, it is now. If there was ever a time to be the change you desire to see in the world, it is now. If there was ever a time to rid yourself of the fear to act, the pride that hinders, and the greed that destroys, it is now. If there was ever a time to get immunized against the outbreak of complaining about everything, of blaming other people for everything and of making excuses in every situation, it is now. If there was ever a time the world needs every hands on deck to make it a better place for the younger generations, to pave way for the downtrodden, the depraved, the discouraged, the depressed, and the dying, it is now. If there was ever a time, a time when we need to wake up from our spiritual slumber and stand up for the peace, love, unity and harmony that we desire, it is now!

Until you realize that the accomplishment of anything has more to do with your mindset than your efforts, you will labour in vain. To accomplish whatever goal, you must first change your mindset. You must first believe in yourself and then in your ability to accomplish the goal. It is this change in mindset that will generate the passion, sharpen the skills and muster the resources that are required to accomplish the goal. Until this change in mindset occurs, nothing else will. Until you can grasp it with your mind, you can never grasp it with your hands.

It is no doubt that some parents have failed their children. It is no doubt that some of those who were elected to lead have failed their electorates. But must we fail others as well? Must we fail ourselves too? Due to pride, stubbornness and self-pity, many of us unfortunately dismiss opportunities to develop patience during opposition, perseverance during oppression, love during hate, joy during trials, and humility during confrontation. Some of us have even used challenges to excuse ourselves from the path of greatness, claiming to be at the lowest level of life because of issues that are not new under the sun. Regardless of how bad, there is nothing new under the sun. Greatness awaits only the peaceful, patient and perseverant.

According to James Allen, "By your own thoughts you make or mar your life, your world, your universe. As you build within by the power of thought, so will your outward life and circumstances shape themselves accordingly. Whatsoever you harbour in the inmost chamber of your heart will sooner or later, by the inevitable law of reaction, shape itself in your outward life. The soul that is impure, sordid, and selfish is gravitating with unerring precision toward misfortune and catastrophe; the soul that is pure, unselfish, and noble is gravitating with equal precision toward happiness and prosperity. Every soul attracts its own. Nothing can possibly come to it that does not belong to it. To realize this is to recognize the universality of divine law. The incidents in every human life, which both make and mar, are drawn to it by the quality and power of its own inner thought-life. Every soul is a complex combination of gathered experiences and thoughts, and the body is but an improvised vehicle for its manifestation. What, therefore, your thoughts are, that is your real self; and the world around you, both animate and inanimate, wears the aspect with which your thoughts clothe it".

To welcome greatness into your life, you must wake up and take back control of the only thing you can be in control of; that is, your mind. You must begin to intently and intimately listen to your conscience once again. You must become open to words of wisdom regardless of how challenging they may be. While you may have been a victimized spectator in the unfortunate circumstances of your childhood, you are now a major player in every circumstance that you find yourself as an adult, whether fortunate or unfortunate. If you only knew the power of Him who is in you, the power of the mind within you, you would never complain of being unable to move your mountains, face your giants, weather your storms, or overcome your obstacles.

When I began my journey en route to fulfillment over a decade ago, I knew it was going to be a tough challenge. So the very first thing I did was to make up my mind to go ahead with it no matter what. This is the first and most important step in whatever you are pursuing in life–to make a decision to remain on the journey no matter what. The next thing I did was to make a list of the top things that I often did to satisfy my tumultuous ego, which I knew were not right. Breaking these habits was harder than anticipated, so I had to, once again, draw on the power of the mind. I made up my mind to stop doing these things immediately without excuses. This had a direct impact on the level of comfort that I was used to, especially since my tumultuous ego, which I had been nurturing all along, was suddenly now left to fend for itself.

My ego was furious and kept applying pressure on me to nurture it. To avoid succumbing to the pressure, I leveraged what I refer to as Absolute Power, which will be discussed later on in this book. I prayed hard, hastily removed myself from the midst of those who were up to no good, and placed myself in the midst of spiritually-minded people. Furthermore, I formed a Band of Encouragers, which was made up of people who were on their own individual journey en route to fulfillment, people who did not mind slowing down to lend me a helping hand along the way; people who were selfless enough to rebuke me when I strayed, exhort me when I lazed, and encourage me when I struggled.

In all these, I learnt that when you make up your mind about something, no one else can hold you back but you. In order to take back control of your mind, painful sacrifices must be made. It may require you to change your whole set of friends, quit your satisfying job or even move to a new territory to start afresh. I had to do all these. You must be willing to give up something to gain something. The sacrifice will hurt, but like in all cases of eventual fulfillment, hurting comes before healing.

What about you? What are the challenges that you anticipate in your journey en route to fulfillment? What are the fears and challenges that may be holding you back right now from welcoming greatness into your life? Spend some time to meditate and reflect on your life and identify the concepts you must unlearn and relearn; the opportunities to be real based on absolute control of you mind rather than going through life under the influence of unfortunate childhood experiences. I have learnt that the mind of a man is like a seabed of inestimable diamonds waiting to be mined. The decisions you make today will steer the direction of your life tomorrow.

Depending on the pain you experienced as a child, the hurt and abuse, it is understandable that this may be a daunting task for you. It was for me. In fact, the excruciating pain of the unpleasant memories may even be making you to live in denial–denial that you were never abused when deep down in your heart you know you were; denial that you were never neglected and abandoned by your parents when deep down in your heart you know you were; denial that you were unloved, uncared for, unwanted, undesired, unsupported, untrained, and the list goes on and on. While it is unfortunate that some of us were put through so much pain at such tender ages, we do not have to succumb to the detrimental impacts. We do not have to allow the atrocities of other people to hinder us from returning to love, from beginning our journey en route to fulfillment, from welcoming greatness into our lives.

Without minimizing the pain of our childhood, there is always someone whose childhood is more pitiable than ours. Having being viciously abused, mentally and physically for reasons that were never really explained to me, I thought my childhood was the most pitiable until I met people who were sexually abused by their parents or siblings every day of their childhood, until I heard of women whose children were fathered by their own fathers, until I heard of people whose mothers made numerous attempts to intentionally have them killed. While it is wise to cause pain to no one, it is still one of those precious gifts of life that presents rare opportunities to grow. If you judge it by its packaging alone, you would not want it. But explore the contents in the package, and you will find nuggets of wisdom that are meant to prepare you for the greater pains that life will definitely deliver to you in due time.

Whether you fall into one of these very unfortunate categories or not, no one is able to comprehend the pain you must have felt, the pain you probably still feel in your heart today. Researches are beneficial to understand the impact of such awful experiences, but it is only the victims who know exactly the pain they went through. In the same way, it is only the victims who can withdraw themselves from the brink of the devastating impact of these despicable childhood experiences like I had to do over a decade ago. Regardless of how painful our childhood experiences were, we always have our adulthood to redeem ourselves. And the time to do so is now.

Whichever way you look at it, there is nothing fundamentally wrong with how we end up becoming based on our childhood experiences. There is something gravely wrong, however, if we choose to neither acknowledge the detrimental impact of these childhood experiences nor make the fundamental changes that are necessary to enhance our mindset moving forward. There is something seriously wrong when we are not willing to overcome the fear, shame, guilt and insecurity that are obviously inherent in our unfortunate childhood experiences, when we are not even willing to begin the journey of healing, our journey en route to fulfillment.

Show me a man with no legs or arms, a man who is deaf, dumb and blind, a man who is neither able to smell nor feel; in a worse predicament is a man who is whole and yet has no self-control. In a worse predicament is a man who is unable to control his mind from gravitating towards evil, to control his tongue from lashing out at other people, and to control his limbs from acting aimlessly. Our genetics, upbringing and environment may have a lot to do with how we naturally think and act, but how we actually think and act are the direct outcomes of the choices we make. How we act during pressures and challenges is an outcome that we are 100% responsible for. Genetics may be likened to a loaded gun, but we are 100% responsible for pulling the trigger. Despite all the dramas in our lives, our upbringing was meant to bring us up and not to bring us down. This is why it is called upbringing and not down-bringing!

To take back control of your mind, you must consistently explore all options and exhaust all avenues. No stone should be left unturned, no excuse should be considered, no time should be wasted, no opportunity should be ignored, no knowledge should be dismissed, and those with the potential of helping should be approached. Above all else, you must exhibit unabashed faith, contagious passion, unwavering integrity, utmost diligence and hearty contentment. Prepare a list of habits and tendencies that are deterring you from welcoming greatness into your life and waste no time in taking the necessary action to become self-controlled. Get a Life Coach if deemed necessary. See a Psychologist if the hurts are that deep.

If you are one of those who always wait for people to change their ways before you change yours, you will never change your ways. If you are one of those who always wait to acquire everything before making the time to do something, you will never do anything. If you are one of those who always wait for everything to be in place before making a move, you may as well remain where you are. If you wish to excel in life, you must be open and willing to learn, unlearn and relearn what is required to make things happen. You must be willing to apply the due diligence, uphold the expected integrity, and go the extra mile consistently. Until you begin your personal journey en route to fulfillment, you are only a captive of yourself and no one else.

Only a few things are harder than owning up to our own inadequacies, than accepting the fact that we may have either lost our mind or have no control over it at all. But when we eventually summon the courage that is necessary to face ourselves, our fears will begin to dissipate, for the giant we are often scared of facing is, in essence, ourselves. After a decade of living an empty life of self only, a series of unfortunate events forced me to examine my pitiable life, my never-ending desires and my self-destructive ego. As I matured in the spirit and in my relationship with God, I realized that those pitfalls, even while excruciating at the time, were certainly necessary to awaken the giant in me. The time to awaken the giant in you is now.

Almighty God,

Since the creation of the world your invisible qualities–your eternal power and divine nature–have been clearly seen, being understood from what has been made, so that we are without excuse. Your power and might is as obvious in the universe as it is when we consider the complexity of our being, the power of our mind. You have graciously created us with everything we need and trustingly gave us the power to do anything we want.

Forgive my thoughts, words and actions that do not bring you glory. Forgive me for not making enough effort to be in control of my mind; forgive me for the regrettable things that I could have avoided had I made enough effort to be in control of my mind. In a world where many people are out of their mind, Lord, a world where many people have either lost their mind or traded it for the pleasures of the world, I thank you for your amazing patience, your overwhelming tolerance, and your never-ending grace. Your love and mercy for us, Almighty Father, is evident across the universe.

Please help me to secure my mind; to protect it from being polluted by the evil of nowadays. Help me, Lord, to recognize the power of my mind and to use it to make the world a better place. Lord, please help the people who are willing to take back control of their minds for the betterment of mankind, and open the eyes of those who are walking on the path that leads to nowhere. May more and more people begin to recognize the power within them, may they wake up from their spiritual slumber to begin their individual journey en route to fulfillment.

Grant us the strength and wisdom to continue making the necessary effort to welcome greatness into our lives.

Amen.

Chapter 2

Inconvenient Truth

"The truth that makes men free is for the most part the truth which men prefer not to hear."

~ Herbert Agar

One of the hardest things to face in life is the ultimate truth about ourselves. It is to accept the pains that would make us look weak and to acknowledge the inadequacies that would make us look ignorant. It is to openly admit to our weaknesses and allow other people to know the true level of our ignorance. And if we are yet to take back control of our mind, then facing ourselves is completely out of the question. In fact, until we begin our individual journey en route to fulfillment, we will feel challenged by confrontations that are necessary, be unresponsive towards knowledge that stands to benefit us, and be defensive against advice that we should desperately seek.

Truth is the quality of being true, genuine, actual, or factual. It is a proven or verified principle or statement. While anyone would gladly say the truth when it is convenient to do so, not many people would dare say or accept the truth when it is inconvenient, when it exposes their nonchalance, ignorance and arrogance. Truth suddenly becomes inconvenient when it is likely to bring our dark side to light, flush out our deepest thoughts and ungodly schemes, or create embarrassment for anyone. It must be such a terrible feeling to suddenly realize that you know everything about yourself but the truth about yourself. Yet we live in a world where the amount of effort wastefully expended by many people everyday to suppress the truth is enough to change the course of our planet from hate to love, from war to peace.

Acknowledging the unfortunate experiences of our childhood falls into this category of inconvenient truth, for how many of us are really comfortable with talking about the abuse we went through as children? How many of us would admit even to ourselves the fact that the abuse we went through in our childhood may have made us become ignorant about the things that really matter in life, and unaware of the basic life skills that are necessary to maintain exhilarating relationships? The fact that we may not want to face it does not mean it did not happen. In fact, the earlier we accept the truth, the easier it is to accept. To welcome greatness into our lives, it is necessary to establish the inconvenient truth about ourselves, and to determine the detrimental impact that is inherent in it. It is imperative that we make consistent effort to release ourselves from the overwhelming shadow of the inconvenient truth.

Are you perceived by others as prideful, selfish, irritating, short-tempered, overindulging, undisciplined, unaccountable, uncompassionate, irresponsible, apprehensive, rude, passive, arrogant, depressed, immature, nonchalant, disrespectful, defiant, forgetful, argumentative, defensive, busybody, impulsive, disorganized, anxious, insatiable, indecisive, rebellious or inconsiderate? Are you struggling with maintaining long-term relationships, with being intimate with your spouse, or with saying no to your children's never-ending requests? Are you uncomfortable with asking others for help, with accepting compliments from others, or with expressing appreciation to others? It is high time that you faced the inconvenient truth.

Are you known to never complete a task, to often buy what is not needed, or to hardly fulfill your promises? Are you comfortable with loneliness, very resistant to change and quickly distracted? Are you perceived to be in self-denial, to procrastinate too much, to distrust others too quickly and to be insecure about yourself? Are there recurring issues in your marriage, parenting, leadership and other relationships with friends, partner, parents, siblings, coworkers, boss, employees and neighbours? Do you wish to be more loving, more open, more vulnerable and more intimate with your spouse? Do you long to be joyful, patient, kind, compassionate, spiritual, relatable, reliable, self-confident, committed, understanding, satisfied, fulfilled, accommodating and assertive?

If you find yourself consistently struggling with any of these character challenges, then it is high time that you summoned the courage to open the baggage of your upbringing and carefully examine the contents therein; your strengths and weaknesses, the propellers of success and deterrents of fulfillment within you. You must be willing to face yourself, take control of your mind, and seek the counselling, coaching and mentorship that is necessary for you to release yourself from the overwhelming shadow of the unfortunate experiences of your childhood. To rid yourself of these deterrents of fulfillment, you must first admit the inconvenient truth. Until then, you will remain a captive of yourself. How else do you expect to get rid of something without first admitting that it exists?

According to M. Scott Peck, "The tendency to avoid problems and the emotional suffering inherent in them is the primary basis of all human mental illness. Since most of us have this tendency to a greater or lesser degree, most of us are mentally ill to a greater or lesser degree, lacking complete mental health. Some of us will go to quite extraordinary lengths to avoid our problems and the suffering they cause, proceeding far afield from all that is clearly good and sensible in order to try to find an easy way out, building the most elaborate fantasies in which to live, sometimes to the total exclusion of reality". This is an inconvenient truth; a fact that, though hard to swallow, must be acknowledged should you wish to welcome greatness into your life.

Until you acknowledge the unfortunate experiences of your childhood, you will be oblivious to the obvious detrimental impacts to your adulthood. Until you seek the counselling, coaching and mentoring that is required to deal with the detrimental impact of your childhood experiences, your life will be troubled and your future will even be more challenging; your relationships will suffer and you will eventually be alone in a world of about seven billion people. Until you are able to face yourself, you will be unable to face other people. Until you are able to understand yourself–why you think and act the way you do–you will always be annoyed and frustrated over the actions of other people. Happiness, you may have intermittently, but you will be unable to experience joy. You will be unable to welcome greatness into your life.

After taking back control of my mind, I had to face the inconvenient truth. I had to accept that some of the hurtful experiences of my childhood had severely impeded my psychological development. This was my inconvenient truth–to realize that I was a psychologically underdeveloped adult. Like Michael Levy once said: "You can bend it and twist it. You can misuse and abuse it. But even God cannot change the Truth." I had to admit that I had been subduing the pain that is inherent in the unfortunate experiences of my childhood. I had to acknowledge my hurts before I could submit them to God for healing. There was no way that I could have begun my journey en route to fulfillment without first having to release myself from the valley of hate, foothill of irresponsibility, ocean of selfishness, mountain of fear, crossroad of uncertainty and the shadow of death. I had to face myself for what I had become to better understand what was required to begin my journey en route to fulfillment.

What is your inconvenient truth? Is it that you were physically or sexually abused as a child by someone in authority, which is now making it difficult for you to be intimate with your loved ones? Is it that you were neglected or abandoned in your childhood, which resulted in you becoming a psychologically underdeveloped adult with a mental capacity that is way below what is expected in your age group? Is it the high level of hypocrisy that you saw in your parents while growing up, which has now made you to become suspicious of everyone in your life? Is it that you were consistently bullied and made to perform shameful acts against your will, which has now made you to become overly defensive even against friendly advice? The rebellion of my youth, which nearly got me killed on numerous occasions, was more due to my unwillingness to admit the inconvenient truth than anything else. I have now learnt that regardless of the pain we go through in life, joy always awaits those who are willing to confront their fears.

When I think of the people that hurt me the most in my life, the people that betrayed me to the point of emotional breakdown, I cannot help but be compassionate towards them because I now know that the pains they caused me were just fractions of the pains they were caused by other people as well. Would someone in his right mind sexually abuse his daughter? Would someone who is in control of his mind physically abuse his children to the point of near death? Would someone who is in control of his mind teach his children how to tell lies? If we were to make everyone pay for the pain they inflicted on other people, even those who play the victim would not escape the judgement. I will forever remain grateful for the example Jesus Christ set while being crucified on the cross. He looked into heaven and asked God to forgive His executors for they did not know what they were doing. So who am I to hold a grudge against any one after having been forgiven so much for my countless atrocities?

Regardless of your academic achievements, vast network and available resources, your success in life and business are directly related, not only to your physical development, but also to your mental capability, emotional stability and spiritual foundation. It is directly related to your ability to identify and manage your emotions based on the present and without prejudice. It is based on your ability to not feel insecure when your space is being invaded, your ignorance exposed, your decisions challenged, your apology requested, and your thoughts provoked. The more you refuse to accept the inconvenient truth about yourself, the less you become of yourself.

While many people wish that their childhood were full of sweet memories, of consistently caring and respectful parents who remarkably loved each other, always expressed compassion, patience and appreciation at every opportunity; parents who worked hard without short-changing family time; parents who were so involved in their academic and extra curricular activities, and sacrificially made time to teach and exemplify life skills and morals like dedication, integrity and servitude, some statistics indicate that it was not so for up to a groundbreaking 95% of the people that were surveyed in some societies. Basically, most of us grew up without really growing up, which is why many people are ill-equipped to effectively manage the challenges they face in their lives. To deny the truth, I have learnt, does not necessarily make it a lie.

It is detrimental to go through life harbouring the pain of unfortunate experiences in life, to be continuously regretful of our past, to always dwell on the insults of others, to consistently complain about the obstacles that we feel are undeserved. But overcoming so much in life is actually a solid foundation for becoming so much in life. And until we begin to reap the benefits of the unfortunate situations that we have been through in life, we would have resigned ourselves to a state of perpetual incapacitation rather than living life to the fullest. We would be giving up our right to joy and peace, our opportunities to welcome greatness into our lives.

Healing only begins to occur when we acknowledge the unfortunate experiences of our upbringing, when we summon the courage to seek the counselling, coaching and mentorship which is necessary to deal with the detrimental impacts of our unfortunate childhood experiences. Until we face the inconvenient truth, the healing process will not begin. Until the healing process begins, we will not be able to forgive those who likely knew not what they were doing. And without forgiveness, there is no healing. Forgiveness was another challenging concept for me to accept, especially since hate, revenge, anger, and malice were what I was inadvertently taught while growing up. I knew people who were still holding grudges with other people who had passed on! What a pitiable way to live; to allow the dead to be in control of your mindset!

In my journey en route to fulfillment, I have learnt that until we truly forgive those who hurt us in the past, we will not be able to truly live in the present. We will not be able to be truly trusting, consistently confident, and deeply affectionate. We will not be able to fully take back control of our mind and bring lasting peace to our soul. We will not be a pleasure to be around. We will neither be a true friend to others nor have true friends to count on. Until we face the inconvenient truth, we will neither be able to begin our journey en route to fulfillment nor welcome greatness into our lives. The only way we can be free enough to attract fulfillment is to let go of the grievances that we have against others. Until then, we would have impeded our growth forever.

Researches indicate many detrimental emotional impacts on people who are abused during their formative years. For example, since alcoholism is a disease of denial, that is, those suffering from it often refuse to admit that they are affected by it, adults whose parents were alcoholics, in turn, often live in self-denial themselves. A research concluded that, "Childhood is abbreviated for children whose parents are alcoholics. They learn to parcel out feelings to avoid upsetting the alcoholic parent or to avoid being held responsible for triggering a bout of parental drinking. The manner in which the child relates and responds is too often determined by the state of the alcoholic, which can be rather unpredictable. The entire family is, in fact, engaged in a struggle to control an uncontrollable situation.

As a result, the methods utilized by affected children to cope with their parent's alcoholism initiates a variety of behaviour which inevitably proceeds into adulthood. The related problems of behaviour and adaptation are often not distinguishable for ten or twenty years. Even in maturity, these individuals tend to be unable to trust their own perceptions or feelings. Often, they continue to deny, (just as their parents had), that anything is wrong. Adult children of alcoholics often doubt their ability to control both themselves and their relationships. Most recent data suggests that concordance for alcoholism in parents is a potent risk factor for the development of antisocial personality-conduct disorder in children. Due to the fact that their lives were in concurrent states of turmoil and confusion when they were children, they often believe that the mere expression of commonplace and normal emotions (i.e. anger, joy, etc) indicates that they lack control.

The manner of coping as children permits affected individuals to survive as adults in a seemingly 'normal' fashion, for quite a while. However, crises begin generally in their late twenties. Very often, these adults do not relate their problems to having grown up with an alcoholic parent. They become depressed and dissatisfied with life, without understanding why. They lack an appropriate perspective of normal behaviour and have no concept of their power to alter this situation because the people who were supposed to be responsible for them as children, (their parents), were not. Therefore, the adult child of an alcoholic has difficulty in identifying needs and/or expressing feelings. They also have substantial fears regarding proper responses and social behaviours which date back to their youth."

Adults who were sexually abused by someone in authority, like a parent, relative, teacher, and community or religious leader are even more impacted emotionally. When someone who was meant to cater for you and protect you no matter what violates you sexually, it results in a series of emotional impacts that severely impede psychological development. Like the children with alcoholic parents, your childhood was abbreviated as well, and the baggage of your upbringing will be full of the tools, which, though you had used to survive and protect yourself throughout your very unfortunate childhood ordeal, now portrays you as cold and conniving. Prominent amongst these self-destructive tools are distrust, denial and depression.

Some researches concluded that the most commonly experienced impact of sexual abuse is posttraumatic stress disorder (PTSD). This type of stress falls into three categories: re-enactment of the event, avoidance or withdrawal, and physiological hyper-activity. Each child is different and may experience any or all of these in various degrees of behaviour. The research further stated that, "A frequent problem with sexual abuse is that the child engages in more sexualized behaviour compared to children who are not sexually abused. Since the abuse took place on and in the body, the body becomes the enemy. They carry a great deal of pain and memories. They desperately try to cope with the pain which can lead to eating disorders, self-inflicting injuries, inability to have sex, or engaging in sex often, poor body image, generalized separation from and disregard for one's body, disassociation, sexual impurity, and gender-identity issues.

Survivors who live through the impact of childhood sexual abuse may have difficulty knowing where their personal boundaries are, how to maintain them, and how to protect themselves from those who do not respect or try to violate their boundaries. They are then vulnerable to further abuse. Trust becomes a very big issue. Trust is harder to develop when the person who abused the child is a caregiver. The abuser is often someone who has a close relationship with them and should be someone the child can trust. Problematic coping behaviours include addictions, prostitution, overworking, inability to work, high-functioning, low-functioning, argumentative, avoiding conflict, perfectionism, wanting to please others.

There are also many emotional effects such as helplessness, feeling dirty, confusion, powerlessness, and pain. Victims may display these emotions by invalidating them, saying, 'It wasn't so bad; it didn't really hurt.' This is a way of self-protection leading to self-blame and self-hatred. Negative self image perspectives come into play with 'I am bad, no one loves me, no one could love me, I am unlovable, and dirty. It's my fault, I am horrible.' The negative effects of incest, the most common form of sexual abuse, can be compounded by the reactions of parents, siblings, and other important people in the child's life. Sometimes siblings of the survivor blame the abused child, either because they believe the perpetrator's denials, or simply because of what reporting the abuser has done to the family. And when a child wonders if her mother knew about the abuse but did nothing to stop it, she can lose trust in both parents, not just one."

The most difficult change to effectuate in life is a personal change in character. It is to revolutionize a way of being and mindset that has been influenced by unfortunate experiences, indecent exposures and inappropriate education. It is to sustain a new way of being which is contradictory to what is generally expected based on abusive upbringing, dangerous environment, and even genetics codes. It did not take me long into my journey en route to fulfillment to realize that the tools which I had devised to protect myself from abuse as a child were no longer required as an adult. It did not take me long to realize that those tools, while required to protect myself then, had become the weapons I was using to destroy the meaningful relationships in my life.

What a relief it was for me to realize that I no longer had to always prove myself to anybody; that I no longer had to accept being abused; that I no longer had to be so defensive, arrogant, or conniving. What a relief it was for me to know that it was more important to live my life in ways that are pleasing to God than it was to live for the praises of other people. What are the tools that you devised for yourself as a child but are now destroying your relationships and hindering you from welcoming greatness into your life? What are the reliefs that you seek in your life so you are able to properly sleep at night? What are the pains of your past that are still causing you pain today? What is the inconvenient truth that you are struggling to admit to yourself?

I have learnt that until we are able to accept the inconvenient truth about ourselves, willing to experience the final leg of the pain that is necessary to heal the wounds of our unfortunate childhood experiences, the maturity gap between our physical and mental beings would gradually widen, making us way less mature in wisdom than in age. Until we start unpacking the baggage of our childhood and begin to deal with the detrimental impact of our childhood experiences, we will remain psychologically underdeveloped adults or, worst still, emotional cripples. An emotional cripple is someone who, due to a lengthy period of physiological abuse in life, has an emotional problem that prevents him or her from expressing feelings of hurt, desire, appreciation, love, etc, that are necessary to have mature conversations and meaningful relationships.

Until you start unpacking the baggage of your childhood and begin to deal with the detrimental impact of your unfortunate childhood experiences, your children will likely lack sense of directions in life as well, before they prematurely become emotionally independent because you lack deep relationship with them. They will likely struggle with expressing appreciation, and see no reason to pursue personal growth and spiritual foundation without you being the example you are meant to be. And if the level of anger, rage, disgust and anguish that remembering these sad childhood experiences still brings out of you is high, they would never know what it means to be truly loved, trusted and appreciated. You would have pitiably succeeded in making them experience a mutated version of the pain you went through as a child.

In the words of Marianne Williamson, "It has become popular these days to blame practically everything on our parents. We figure it is because of them that our self-esteem is so low. However, if we take a closer look at how our parents treated us, whatever abuse they gave us was often mild compared to the way we abuse ourselves today. It is true that your mother might have repeatedly said, 'You'll never be able to do that, dear.' Now you say to yourself, 'You're a jerk. You never do right. You blew it. I hate you.' They might have been mean, but we are vicious". If we were failed by those who claim to love us, must we also fail those who we claim to love?

Whatever happened to you in the past to now make you struggle emotionally, to now put you below the level of mental capability that is expected of someone in your age group, will never sit well with you. Trying to make sense out of it and trying to understand and comprehend it will continue to cause you more emotional damage. Burying it in your heart altogether with no intention of bringing it to light is like putting a time bomb under your bed while you sleep. It was not easy for me as well, nor was it for those who also made up their mind to courageously unpack the baggage of their upbringing. But when you eventually decide to face the inconvenient truth, you will become lighter, liberated and lively. I have learnt that to embark on your journey en route to fulfillment, it is imperative that you first deal with the emotional challenges that are inherent in the unfortunate experiences of your childhood.

Rather than a physical check-up, mental, emotional and spiritual check ups are what many of us need to perform on a regular basis. When we focus on our issues, they will never go away. Through Prophet Jeremiah, God affirmed that He created us with plans to prosper us and not to harm you, plans to give us hope and a future. Thus, if we are not experiencing these in our lives, we may not be heading the right direction. I have learnt that until we give up our hurts and pains, God will not take them up. It is only until we surrender the matter to God that it will no longer matter to us. I have learnt that disability is more of a mental limitation than a physical one, more of an attitude than appearance. It is when we are bent on doing things when and how we want things done despite the negative impact on others.

Over a decade into my journey en route to fulfillment, I have learnt that despite the ugliness of the world, we are beautiful within, that despite the weakness of the body we are powerful within. Admitting the inconvenient truth is the beginning to a whole new mindset that is necessary to welcome greatness into your life. If we only knew the power that exists within us, we would never complain of being unable to conquer our challenges. If we only knew the impact that we were created to make in this world, we would look to no one else but ourselves for the change we desire in the world. Regardless of how small your faith may seem to you, call forth that miracle of healing with all the faith you have and then prepare to be abundantly blessed.

The ultimate truth is that we are the most important creation of all creations, the glue that was created to hold other creations together, and the conductor of whatever happens to other creations. We have the most important assignment on earth and a direct access to our Creator in heaven. We are powerful beyond measure, durable beyond understanding, and flexible beyond explanation. Our past is forgiven, our present is secure, and our future is certain. We are endowed with the privileges of being God's Ambassador here on earth, and honoured to carry His Holy Spirit within us. All animals and plants, whether at sea, on land, or in the air are subject to us, are dependent on our mercy and compassion. With our mouth, we can praise or prick anyone. With our eyes, we can regard or disregard anything. With our limbs, we can build or destroy. With our heart, we can love or hate our fellow human beings.

The power to encourage or discourage anyone is in our hands. The power to be whatever we choose to be and do whatever we choose to do is in our hand regardless of the inconvenient truth, regardless of whatever situation we find ourselves in life. To welcome greatness into our lives, we must humbly accept this glorious position. We must willingly assume these honourable responsibilities regardless of how daunting they may be. It is only then that our past will be forgiven, our present will be secure, and our future will be certain. It is only then we would be confident of the love and support of our Creator, now and forevermore.

Almighty God,

I come before you broken; broken from the hurts of my past, the impact of one abuse or the other in my past. I come before you in search of peace of mind, in search of the love that I have been denied for so long by some of the people you put in my life.

I come before you in awe of your grace, your love and the blessings which you continue to shower upon me despite my doubts of your love, despite the anger, resentment and even hatred that I may be harbouring towards those who have caused me pain. I come before you, Father, to escape the ugliness of the world and the weakness of my body.

Here I am, Lord, to worship and accept you into my life, to submit to your will for my life. Please give me the courage to open the baggage of my upbringing and the wisdom to deal with the contents therein. There are some things in there which I am in denial of, which I refuse to admit, to acknowledge and to accept. Help me to carry my cross to Calvary, Lord, in my journey en route to fulfillment. Father, Lord, as I work towards welcoming greatness into my life, I welcome you as my Partner, my Guide, and my Protector.

I welcome your company, Lord; I welcome you into my life and now look forward to an exciting road trip with you, my Lord, my Saviour. I now look forward to dwelling in the bosom of your love on this exciting journey that will eventually enable me to welcome greatness into my life.

Thank you, Lord, for always listening to me even when I am not praying.

Amen.

Chapter 3

Absolute Power

> **"Faith consists in believing when it is beyond the power of reason to believe."**
>
> **~ Voltaire**

When we appreciate the magnitude of the task at hand, attempting to do it all alone would not even be an option. Physical tasks, we may attempt alone depending on our physical strength, but mental, emotional and spiritual tasks were never meant to be assumed alone especially if we wish to welcome greatness into our life and sustain our journey en route to fulfillment. Absolute Power is the combination of the power within us, the power in others, and the Power of God. By our individual selves, we can do so much, but when we tap into the power in those around us, while drawing on power directly from God as well, there is no limit to what we can do.

Absolute Power is a concept that expands on the popular concept of self-reliance; that is, the popular notion that within each individual exists power beyond measure, and that we can draw on this power within us to make things happen in our lives. Absolute Power takes you a couple of steps higher than this limited notion. According to Ella Wheeler Wilcox, "The great secret and central fact of the universe is that there exists a Spirit (Intelligent Energy) of Infinite Life and Power that is back of all, that animates all, and from which all comes. And to the degree that we come to a realization of this Infinite Source and learn to connect ourselves with it, do we make it possible for this power to work within us, to manifest through us. What you call this 'Infinite Source' or 'Intelligent Energy' is up to you. But there is no denying that it exists. It is where Your Life Power comes from, for you to use (or not use) as you choose."

Contrary to general perception, greatness is less about our individual ability to make things happen and more about our willingness to work with and through others to make things happen. It is less about us believing only in ourselves and more about us equally believing in other people as well as in a Divine Power that has control over everything within or outside our control. When I reminisce about the challenges I have conquered in my journey en route to fulfillment, it would be remiss on my part to not acknowledge the divine assistance that I received through the certain people that God had graciously placed on my paths. It would be very foolish of me to have gotten the help that I needed and exactly when I needed it and then attribute it to chance.

How else would we ever accomplish anything if we did not believe in ourselves and in the people who possesses the skills that are required to make things happen? How else would we ever accomplish anything if we did not believe that the forces of nature would cooperate favourably to ensure success in our endeavours? How else would we ever be able to break through life's never-ending challenges, break out of the limited thinking that is inherent in unfortunate childhood experiences, and break into the pool of knowledge that was left behind by sages of the past? If God did not think we needed the support of one another, he would not have blessed us with the means of procreation. Even in my days of rebellion, I needed the support of people to achieve my devious plans. And now, considering that my journey en route to fulfillment requires me to consistently suppress my natural tendencies of nonchalance, arrogance and ignorance, I need all the support I can get including that of God Himself!

To welcome greatness into our lives, we must believe in ourselves and in the people whose destinies may be to help us welcome greatness into our lives. We must be willing to acknowledge that there are people and things we have no control over and yet hope work out in our favour. We must be willing to lead and be led, feed and be fed, love and be loved, trust and be trusted, care and be cared for. We must be willing to surrender our doubts, fears and guilt. We must be willing to put in 100% thought and effort into 100% of everything we do. We must pray consistently and hope unswervingly that the things which are outside our control will work to our favour, and then, we must leave the unknown for our Almighty God to take care of.

According to James Allen: "When farmers have tilled and dressed the land and put in the seed, they know that they have done all that they can possibly do and that they now must trust to the elements and wait patiently for the course of time to bring about the harvest, and that no amount of expectancy on their parts will affect the results. Even so, they who have realized truth go forth as sowers of the seeds of goodness, purity, love, and peace, without expectancy and never looking for results, knowing that there is the great overruling law that brings about its own harvest in due time and which is alike the source of preservation and destruction." There was no way I could have unlearned 27 years worth of limited thinking all by myself, without the help of God through those who were ahead of me in the journey en route to fulfillment.

Those who consistently doubt the capabilities of other people will always achieve below their own capabilities. Those who believe that by themselves they can do everything will always end up achieving nothing. While we are to take control of our destiny and run with it, not being open to the guidance and support of other people is a deliberate act to sabotage our own efforts. Dieting and exercising may end up making us healthier, but whether we survive a terminal disease or not is beyond our control and often beyond human understanding. If science truly believed in its sole ability to do and explain all things there would be no need for palliative care in our hospitals. When we become humble enough to tap into Absolute Power, the notions of barriers and limits will disappear. We will be catapulted to a whole new level of maximum living. We will begin to welcome greatness into our lives.

Those who consistently doubt the existence of God are yet to appreciate the complexities of earth, the beauty of the galaxies and the magnitude of the universe. For even the most complex and beautiful things to have ever been created by man only await a disgraceful recall, a painful reengineering, and another doubtful re-launch. The question has never been whether we believe in God or not, but rather whether we are humble enough to accept the fact that we have no control over the ultimate outcome of whatever it is we set out to do. Until we are able to control the weather, explore the greatest depths of the ocean and count the stars in the universe, we better believe. Until we can create a human being without using any part of God's creation, we better believe. Until we can forecast with exactitude what tomorrow holds for everyone in every area of life, we better believe. How guaranteed are you to be alive tomorrow?

Absolute Power is the combined belief in self, in others and in God. It is the humble acknowledgement that by ourselves we can only do so much, but by believing in God and in the power within other people, there is no limit to what we can hope for, what we can achieve. For power to be absolute it must be free of limitations and restrictions. It must be unrestrained and unlimited by any constitution or counterbalancing group. Absolute Power is contained in no one else but God, and yet graciously available to everyone else through each other. It cannot be possessed but rather leveraged at will.

It is Absolute Power that enables us to relentlessly persevere despite major obstacles and stand up for our beliefs despite strong opposition. It is Absolute Power that enables us to consider restrictions and limitations as opportunities for us to demonstrate some of the amazing capabilities that we never even knew existed within us. It is Absolute Power that makes our determination stronger, our effort tireless, our focus sharp, and our faith unabashed. It is Absolute Power that will enable us to welcome greatness into our lives, into our businesses, and into the world.

Telling yourself that you are not good at something greatly increases the likelihood of you ever becoming good at it. Doubting your ability to make a difference in the world limits your self-esteem and creates a chasm between you and greatness. Say what you mean and mean what you say. Always think what you truly want because you will end up pursuing what you often think. Regardless of how it may sound, we actually do call the shots in our lives, for what we strongly believe in, we are often able to make happen. On the contrary, what we strongly doubt, we should not expect to achieve.

Through Absolute Power, I have learnt that we are a unique creation, one of a kind; God has endowed us with a particular mix of talents, abilities, strengths and weaknesses to make a difference.

We were created for a purpose and are blessed with the potentials to achieve that purpose. Our creation was not an accident, but rather a deliberate act of God. We were created by Love to be the epitome of love, by Greatness to be an embodiment of greatness. Not even our thoughts and actions can ever change that. The secret to our success and fulfillment in life is already within us. It is called a secret because it is only us who can find it within ourselves.

Absolute Power is when we are sure that the things beyond our control will work out to our favour regardless of what history and statistics suggest; when we acknowledge that the number of things which are inexplicable is greater than the number of things which are explicable; when we are confident that what we hope for and are certain of would come to pass in miraculous ways; when we believe that "God works in all things for the good of those who love him, those who have been called according to his purpose", as stated by Apostle Paul. To welcome greatness into our lives, we must move away from the notion of self-reliance and self-sufficiency to the ageless concept of faith in God and in the brotherhood, from the notion of the power within us only to the reality of Absolute Power for all to leverage.

If you examine the lives of those who the world unanimously considers to be among the greatest, you will find that they consistently leveraged Absolute Power while other people were fruitlessly struggling to move mountains and break through barriers all by themselves. They believed in themselves, in other people, and in God. It is the same God who created the heroes we look up to that created us as well. Every one of us was created equal and blessed with unique talents. The main difference is that those we classify as heroes chose to maximize their talents for the betterment of the world while the rest of us choose to not maximize ours. It is the same spirit that compelled them to greatness that is compelling us today as well. If we choose to ignore the wakeup call for our journey en route to fulfillment, we should not expect to be fulfilled any other way.

Look at Jesus Christ through whom the world has come to know God. He consistently relied on God through faith and prayers, and in his twelve disciples through faith and encouragement. He relied on his disciples even when he foreknew he was going to be betrayed by one of them! "Truly I tell you", He once said, "if you have faith as small as a mustard seed, you can say to this mountain, 'Move from here to there,' and it will move. Nothing will be impossible for you." The littlest faith you have can conquer the biggest challenge on your path. Call on God with this little faith and you won't believe the miracle that would come forth. I didn't either.

It is Absolute Power that must be leveraged to gain clarity, to manage challenges and to blaze trails. It is Absolute Power that must be leveraged to consistently feel alive, stronger, loved, determined, happier, enthusiastic, joyful, hopeful, energized and eager–even in the midst of chaos. If you are in the pursuit of these qualities without faith, hope and love, your pursuit will be in vain. The control of our mind is unsustainable if it is not connected to Absolute Power, if it not being nourished and encouraged by God and our allies in the journey en route to fulfillment.

What are the mountains you must move, oceans you must cross and giants you must face in order to welcome greatness into your life? What are the challenges you are dealing with, fears you are struggling with, detrimental thoughts you are nurturing, doubts you are entertaining and guilt you are carrying around which are hindering your journey en route to fulfillment? What are the goals you must accomplish, dreams you must pursue and character changes you must make to become an example to those around you, to be able to make an impact so strong that the world will remember you even when you are long gone? It is time for you to leverage Absolute Power.

To welcome greatness into your life, you must begin to build confidence in yourself, have faith in those around you and trust God to bless your effort. The confidence people have in you is a direct reflection of the confidence you have in yourself. When you have no confidence in yourself, doubting even the amazing qualities others see in you, why would you ever expect anyone else to have confidence in you? Why would you expect people to see something good in you when you see nothing good in yourself and in others? Don't you know that we are the heroes we have been waiting for, the people who were created by God to sustain this planet? The people you are looking up to were not created differently than you were, so why are you wasting time sitting still instead of standing up for something worthwhile?

There is nothing great about the notion of self-reliance and self-sufficiency. Having it all and knowing it all has never been the sole criteria for achieving it all. While self-reliance is commendable to a point, it is often based on pride, selfishness, fear, laziness and greed. It often fuels the prideful unwillingness to share opportunities with other people, the selfish unwillingness to allow others share in our breakthroughs. Those who live their lives without leveraging Absolute Power will quickly become stressed, heavy laden and overburdened. They are often consumed with worries and anxieties, which have physical, mental, emotional and spiritual complications. Those who are trying to understand everything, unwisely channelling their efforts towards doing everything all by themselves and trying to be certain of everything and being everything to everyone, will quickly become frustrated, dejected, aggravated and humiliated.

When you leverage Absolute Power, you will feel stronger despite being beaten, exalted despite being betrayed, encouraged despite being insulted and determined despite being oppressed. You will stand firm despite being crushed, satisfied despite being deprived, refreshed despite being burned, motivated despite being discouraged, loved despite being abused and happy despite being bruised. You will feel accepted despite being rejected, hopeful despite being alone, faithful despite being grieved, and, in the words of Apostle Paul, "sorrowful, yet always rejoicing, poor, yet making many rich, having nothing, and yet possessing everything".

It is Absolute Power that must be leveraged to forgive so much, love so dearly, believe so strongly, sing so loudly and pray so passionately. It is Absolute Power that must be leveraged to feel so relieved, so resolved, so refreshed, so redeemed, so reinvigorated and so revived. If you desire any of these without fostering the faith and humility required to believe in what is unseen, your desire will result in nothing. Until we are faithful enough to trust what we may not necessarily understand, we will always find it difficult to trust what we claim to understand. Considering the pain I caused many people during my days of rebellion, nothing but the Power of God and the amazing support of other people could have helped me to overcome the guilt, to embrace forgiveness on both ends, and to become compassionate towards others.

What you need to accomplish your goals in life, to conquer your challenges, and to blaze trails for others to follow may seem overwhelming, but the very first step, the most important step, is to leverage Absolute Power. It is to strengthen your faith in yourself, in the people around you and in God, your Creator. It is this tri-faith that will provide you with the strength and clarity to reach the pinnacle of your existence, to welcome greatness into your life. It was my realization that I will not be travelling alone in my journey en route to fulfillment that strengthened my determination to begin; it is my acquaintance with Absolute Power that energizes my resilience to remain on the road less travelled, that fuels my passion to live a life of purpose until death relieves me of my duty here on earth.

Almighty God,

You are absolutely powerful beyond measure. You are the Creator of the universe and everything in it!

I confess my unbelief . . . in myself, in others and in you. I confess my inability to grasp the magnitude of your Divine Power and the power within me and others. I acknowledge the many times I have thought, spoken and acted in unbelief.

Thank you, Father, for your patience as I work towards believing in Absolute Power. Thank you, Lord, for always watching out for me more than I could ever do for myself. Thank you for the amazing abilities, skills and opportunities that you bestow upon me and for your constant blessing of love, compassion, grace and salvation.

Father, please help me to overcome my unbelief and the lack of confidence that I have in personality, leadership, marriage, parenting, spirituality, relationships, health & wellness, academics, career, finances and business.Help me to believe in myself without a doubt, to believe in others with absolute certainty and to believe in you wholeheartedly.

Father, please open my eyes so that I may see your abounding glory around me. Soften my heart so that I may feel your overwhelming presence around me.

May I think, speak and act with absolute certainty of Absolute Power. I ask these in the name of your Son, Jesus Christ our Lord.

Amen.

Chapter 4

Life of Purpose

> **"The purpose of life is not to be happy–but to matter, to be productive, to be useful, and to have it make some difference that you have lived at all."**
>
> **~ Leo Rosten**

Of all the things that we can be ignorant of, not knowing the ultimate reason for our existence is the most detrimental; not knowing how the things we live for fit into the ultimate plan for mankind is the most unfortunate. And yet, many people in the world today fall into these regrettable categories. It must be tormenting to realize at the end that we made so much effort in life and yet made no impact at all; that we worked so hard and yet contributed nothing significant towards the realization of our life purpose; that we lived so long and yet were unaware of the reason we were created in the first place; that we acquired so much and yet would be leaving no legacy behind. In my journey en route to fulfillment, I have learnt that until we are absolutely sure of our life purpose, and making every effort towards attaining it, we are yet to live.

We live in a world where many people are in the pursuit of things that will only bring temporal satisfaction, things that must be consistently updated and upgraded, renewed and renovated. Many people are currently in careers that consistently increase their network and net worth and yet bring them no peace or joy. Many people live in paramount affluence and yet have no influence over their children. Many people set objectives for themselves and yet have no idea about the eternal consequences of their plans. The cock may crow, the sun may rise, but the day only breaks for those who are willing to live a life of purpose, those who are willing to wake up and stand up for something, those who are willing to make the world a better place for everyone through their examples in life, leadership and love.

While the world may be overly concerned with the possibility of a large asteroid crashing into our planet, the destructive direction of the world is largely due to the waywardness and aimlessness of a growing number of its inhabitants. It is largely due to the high number of people who wake up every morning without relating their daily activities to the reasons they were created in the first place. It is largely due to the high number of people who wake up each morning with plans to do only the bare minimum in everything. And as long as people allow hurt, laziness and pride to deter them from becoming representatives of love, agents of progress and examples of leadership, the world will continue on a destructive direction. But as more people begin to live lives of purpose and take responsibility for the direction of the world, the manpower to make the changes that are so desperately needed will increase.

For many years, I was in pursuit of things that only brought me temporal satisfaction; things that made me look "successful" on the outside but left me completely empty on the inside. I was in the pursuit of what I saw other people pursuing–wealth, fame and power. These were my driving forces, for I thought, like many people still sadly think today, that attaining these things would eventually give me peace and tranquility. Designer clothing, luxury vehicles and prominent "friends" were my motivators, but yet, even after acquiring so much, I still did not have the inner peace and eternal joy which I ignorantly thought would be derived from material possessions. These things satisfied my tumultuous ego but not my hungry spirit. They made people sing my praises but yet pained my conscience at the same time.

It was a great feeling to be able to call the shots in everything around me but a horrible feeling to not be able to call the shots in anything within me. I lived a public life of everything, and privately, a mundane life of nothing. A succession of things brought me temporal satisfaction but yet left me completely empty inside. I lived a life of 'wealth accumulation' rather than that of 'love distribution'. After running a race of desires that led me nowhere for over a decade, I finally realized that despite increasing material possessions, our lives will always be empty until we discover our individual purpose in life and begin to work towards it unswervingly. Many of us travel around the world in search of fulfillment only to return home and realize that it has always been within us. Although through the hard way, I learnt that it is not what "the created" (we) wants that truly matters, but rather what "the Creator" (God) has created us for. Everything else is trivial and irrelevant.

Most of us would agree that the world is too complex for anyone to have been created without a purpose, but yet only a few of us are able to pinpoint our exact purpose in life. When we take a closer look at people who everyone would agree lived lives of purpose, people like Martin Luther King Jr. and Mother Teresa, we would see that all they basically did was to direct their natural talents towards the achievement of supernatural activities, activities that demonstrated love for others, activities that contributed towards making the world a better place. If whatever you are always engaged in does not stand to benefit the people you may never meet, you are yet to begin living a life of purpose.

While Martin Luther King Jr. directed his intelligence, passion and eloquence towards convincing the world that racism is inhumane, Mother Teresa directed her humility, kindness and compassion towards convincing the world to care for the poor. The more I studied examples of those who lived lives of purpose, the more I became convinced that the purpose of life is to enable the life purpose of other people. It is to make other people matter, to make other people count. It is to support the impact that other people are making in the world; to persist in love, to be the change the world desires, and to be yet another example of someone who lived a life of purpose as well.

Until we start making the necessary effort to fulfill our life purpose, working diligently towards making the world a better place each day we have the privilege of living in it, we would have unfortunately given up the unique opportunity to live longer than our physical existence. In fact, death wins when we die without having fulfilled our life purpose, without having accomplished our individual reason for being born. If you are yet to discover yours, look deeply within yourself; search your heart, your mind and your soul for those natural talents that you were blessed with, and then start using those talents to make an impact in your home, workplaces and communities. Pray harder for God to open your eyes to your purpose in life and to grant you the wisdom, passion and strength to pursue your purpose in life no matter what.

Adverse circumstances in our childhood may have robbed us of the desire to live lives of purpose, but the good news is that our purpose in life is in the core of our existence and can never be taken away from us. This is why Nelson Mandela was able to sit in prison for twenty-seven years because he denounced racism and apartheid, because he refused to keep quiet when his fellowmen were unjustly oppressed and enslaved. Which of the unjust situations in your community can you become a voice of reason for? Sometimes, our life purpose is nothing else but to take a stand for something and be willing to die for it. In the words of Martin Luther King Jr., "Until a man finds what he can die for, he is not fit to live". When we truly discover our life purpose, nothing else will matter to us; not even death on a cross!

What are your natural talents and how can you utilize them to make a difference in the lives of those around you? We may not all be called to inspire millions like Martin Luther King Jr. was, but we definitely have a role to play in empowering those around us. Every one of us has an ability to contribute something relatively substantial towards making the world a better place than when we first came into it. Perhaps your purpose in life is to be a source of encouragement for teenaged mothers, which may be why you were once a teenage mother yourself. Perhaps it is to use your scientific mind to invent something that will ensure developing countries have access to clean water, without allowing yourself to be consumed more by the profit than by the impact.

The reason for so many vacuums in a world that is so full of people is that many people are unwilling to assume their designated positions to make the world a better place. Due to fear, laziness or ignorance, some of those who may even know what their natural talents are have convince themselves that other people are more prepared to assume the purpose they were born to fulfill in life. What a pitiable mindset to have. Imagine if the heroes we adore today had left their designated positions in life for others to fill. Imagine if Bill Gate had not taken the leap of faith to quit Harvard University in the pursuit of his dream, if Abraham Lincoln had decided to leave the signing of the Emancipation Proclamation for his successors to deal with, or if Martin Luther King Jr. was not willing to die for his dream.

To live a life of purpose, you must first get out of your own way. You must free yourself from your own limitations; the detrimental thoughts that you are not good enough, not smart enough, not talented enough and not impacting enough. You must acknowledge and appreciate your natural talents, and establish how and where you may start using them to make a difference in the lives of other people. Having been in bondage to material possessions for so many years, the passion in my heart remains to bring messages of hope to the people who are in similar situations, people who have become nonchalant, ignorant or arrogant about what truly matters in life. In my journey en route to fulfillment, I have learnt that we can all be heroes. We just have to start behaving like one without aiming to be one.

A life of purpose may be likened to a marathon because whether we are awake or asleep, we are either running towards something or away from it. A marathon is an event of greater than normal length or duration and requires exceptional endurance to complete. Like a marathon, to live a life of purpose or to succeed in any meaningful endeavour requires exceptional endurance. It requires you to make more effort than you think you can, to push yourself beyond any limit known to you. It requires you to overcome your doubts by faith, confront your fears with courage, and assume your tasks with passion. These are some of the major differences between a race of desires, which I ran for many years, and the marathon of life, which is a life of purpose.

One of the main reasons people live only for themselves rather than for a purpose greater than they are is because their parents likely did the same. When we were children, our choice of profession was often based on our innate dream to make a difference in the lives of other people. This is why we often wanted to be doctors, lawyers, police or fire officers, nurses, teachers, bankers, bakers, or other professions with direct impacts on the lives of other people. But as the list of what we desire in life grew, our focus became easily distorted and we began to confuse our mere desires with the dreams we were created to achieve. In some cases, parents would naively step in to reinforce certain professions because of the prestige and financial reward that are associated with these professions rather than because of the potential impact on mankind, which is our natural way of thinking as children. Perhaps this is why Jesus Christ once said that unless we change and become like little children, we will never enter the kingdom of heaven.

Which of you had parents who wanted you to become a doctor because they were grooming you to work for Doctors without Boarders, which is a non-profit organization that provides urgent medical care to victims of war? Which of you had parents who wanted you to become a lawyer because they were grooming you to become a lawyer who would be known for representing the homeless, downtrodden, dejected and depressed? It is because of such pressure from parents and society that many people sadly gave up the dreams they were created to achieve for the race of desires that leads nowhere.

A desire is a craving, a request, a want, a longing for something that will only bring about temporal satisfaction, while a dream is a succession of images, thoughts or visions that passes through the mind during sleep, and, voluntarily or involuntarily, occurs while awake as well. Defined in some dictionaries as the most ideal of all desires, a dream is intangible, often a stretch of one's capability to achieve, and creates strong feelings of emotions like excitement, anxiety, determination and fear.

While a desire focuses on self, a dream stands to benefit others. While a desire offers temporary satisfaction, a dream offers eternal fulfillment. While a desire is born from our wants, a dream is instilled in us from birth. While a desire goes with the flow, a dream disrupts the flow. While a desire can be suppressed, a dream cannot be suppressed no matter what. While a desire dies when we die, the dream that was placed on our heart at birth will live on forever, even after we pass on. Martin Luther King Jr. may be dead, but his dream for equality for all races continues. Mother Teresa may have passed on, but her dream to bring awareness to the heightened levels of hunger around the world continues. What is the worthy cause that your name would be associated with when you are long gone?

Many of what we call dreams, like exotic vacations and prestigious careers, are mere desires because of the strong likelihood of us realizing them in our lifetimes if we are determined enough. In addition, these desires do not stir the slew of emotions in us like dreams would. Compare your desire for a five-bedroom home with the dream of Martin Luther King Jr., when he said that, "one day on the red hills of Georgia, the sons of former slaves and the sons of former slave owners will be able to sit down together at the table of brotherhood". Compare your desire for fame, power, control, comfort and status, with Mother Teresa's dream to sacrificially leverage all her network and net worth to eradicate poverty in her sphere.

Many of us see the achievements of other people and envyingly convince ourselves that pursuing the same achievements will bring us the fulfillment we desire in life. We find ourselves in the midst of certain people and suddenly feel the inferiority complex for not being as wealthy or healthy as they are. We become so consumed with the desire to be rich, famous and powerful that we completely become oblivious to the natural talents we were blessed with to make the world a better place. In the words of

George Bernard Shaw, "This is the true joy in life, the being used for a purpose recognized by yourself as a mighty one; the being thoroughly worn out before you are thrown on the scrap heap; the being a force of nature instead of a feverish selfish little clod of ailments and grievances complaining that the world will not devote itself to making you happy". What message is your way of life sending to those around you?

As if the unfortunate result of improper parenting is not prevalent enough in our societies, most sitcoms, reality shows, talk shows and commercials unfortunately continues to insinuate that we were created to do what we want, when we want and how we want. How ignorant it is for us to think that we were created by nothing and for nothing. How arrogant it is for us to think that we are all that matters, that we are more important than everyone else. Pursuing the same accomplishments that everyone else is pursuing will never lead you to fill the vacuum that can only be filled when you are in the pursuit of your own dream. Pursuing material possessions at the expense of eternal satisfaction will eventually rob you of joy, peace, harmony and fulfillment.

To welcome greatness into your life, you must consistently ask yourself how your tiny pushes are helping to make the world a better place; you must consistently ask yourself whether you are employing your talents to improve the lives of those around you. Some of us claim to be leaders and yet are consistently the follower in every situation. We claim to be innovative and yet stuff our homes with the innovations of other people. We claim to be spiritual and yet live lives that barely reflect love, joy, peace, patience, kindness, goodness, faithfulness, gentleness and self-control. Many of us have clogged our lives with so many desires that our dreams are no longer obvious to anyone–not even to ourselves! Are you living for what you were created for?

In my journey en route to fulfillment, I have learnt that greatness is only attracted to those who would never go to bed without having questioned their own progress in the marathon of life. To welcome greatness into your life, you must question yourself on a daily basis whether you are running to win a medal that will soon be faded, stolen, misplaced or lost, or whether you are running for the exhilarating feeling and eternal joy that can only be derived from living a life of purpose. Discovering my life purpose was a significant step in my journey en route to fulfillment. It made my path clearer, my direction obvious and my future secure. It was more appealing than the life of 'wealth accumulation' for the eventual consumption of people who don't mean well.

Everyone of us are equipped by God to fulfill our respective life purpose in this world; and shying away from our responsibilities to humanity, whether out of fear, laziness, pride or selfishness, benefits no one. When we create desires for ourselves based on the achievement of others, allowing our action and inaction to be greatly influenced by our surroundings rather than by spirituality, sooner or later, our lives will gradually become void of meaning.

Those who are running the race of desires will gradually wreck their lives before eventually burying themselves amongst the people who left more vacuums in this world by passing on without having fulfilled their purpose in life. I chose to live a life of purpose because I have learnt that what will be said of us when we depart this world will be reflective of our selfishness or selflessness, cowardice or courage, aimlessness or purposefulness. I may die poor, but would have expended all that I am, all that I own for the benefit of mankind.

Within each of us lie the natural talents that we require to achieve our dreams regardless of how monumental we may perceive them to be. Within each of us lie the abilities to fulfill our individual purpose in life regardless of how groundbreaking they may seem to us. The world continues to spend so much time and effort exploring space for new discoveries when within us here on earth lays insurmountable deposits of unique talents waiting to be employed in the fulfillment of our purpose in life.

Within some of us lies the cure for AIDS and other baffling ailments. Within some of us lies the diplomacy that is required to prevent thc breakout of wars and other form of hostility around the world. We must continually mine ourselves to discover our talents in the same way diamonds are mined. We must consistently allow ourselves to be refined by fire to become pure like in the process of refining gold. The key to our success in life lies within us. It lies in knowing our purpose in life and in ensuring that we are on our individual journey en route to fulfillment. Until you are unswervingly living a life purpose, everything else you do will not matter in the end.

Whether we choose to run the marathon of life or the race of desires, our ultimate race has already been marked out for us. The question is not whether we are in the race or not, but rather which direction we are heading in. We may be defensive about the underlying motives of our action and inaction, but as the old saying goes, "time will tell". And eventually, it does. The race of desires is like the Black Hole; it consumes everything on its path and yields nothing in return. The time to begin living a life of purpose is now, for later is a thief of success, a major hindrance to the fulfillment we seek in life. If we only knew the impact we were created to make in this world, we would look to no one else but ourselves for the change we desire in the world.

Almighty God,

Thank you for revealing my life purpose to me, for helping me to realise that, while I may be insignificant when viewed through our natural eyes, you have set me aside for things that are way greater than the world itself.

Thank you, Lord, that I was created by you and for you, that I mean so much to you despite the nonchalance, ignorance and arrogance with which I sometimes approach life. Thank you for the call that woke me up to my purpose in life.

As I continue on my journey en route to fulfillment, I pray that you replenish my strength before it depletes, refresh my wisdom before it expires and soften my heart each and every day. I also pray for those who are currently on their individual journey as well, those who are bent on living their lives for you. Please protect us all from the evil one, from schemes that others may have devised to derail us.

May our eyes be open to see the unseen, hear the unheard and feel the unfelt. Father, please come to the aid of those who are in search of their purpose in life. Help them to be diligent, humble and passionate enough to heed your calling as well. May the number of those stepping up to make the world a better place increase every day, through your Son, our Lord Jesus Christ.

Thank you, Father, for such a humbling opportunity to wake up each day and be blessed with the desire, strength and wisdom to live a life of purpose. May I live long enough and work hard enough to expend my talents, passion and intelligence for the betterment of mankind before I get the honour of returning back to you.

Amen.

Phase 2:

> "Everything that irritates us about others can lead us to an understanding of ourselves."
>
> ~ Carl Gustav Jung

Chapter 5

Acute Imperative

> **"The illiterate of the 21st century will not be those who cannot read and write, but those who cannot learn, unlearn, and relearn".**
>
> **~ Alvin Toffler**

The world is growing more complex by the minute. What we buy today may be outdated tomorrow. The information that is considered truth today may be proven to be a lie tomorrow. What we see before we go to bed at night may be no more by the time we wake up the next morning. What had worked well for ages may be rendered ineffective within the next few minutes. We live in a world where what is valid today often becomes invalid tomorrow–even before it reaches its predetermined lifespan! You drive a vehicle for many years and then it is suddenly recalled for safety issues!

Knowledge is no different. In fact, to cope with ongoing globalization, the demand for higher productivity, depleting natural resources, increasing commodity prices, decreasing wages, need for double income, escalating debt rate, widening socio-economic gap, simultaneous wars, mass immigration, need for impenetrable security, et cetera, we must consistently increase the knowledge we require to better cope with these astronomical changes. In the same way, we must be in consistent pursuit of the knowledge that is required to sustain our journey en route to fulfillment. As much as anything else we consider imperative, we must ensure that our rate of intellectual growth is at least up to par with today's rate of technological change, especially since what students learn in their first year of university is obsolete before they graduate from a four-year degree program! In retrospect, the knowledge that has brought you thus far in life is insufficient to take you to the next level of greatness.

To survive in today's world, we must be in constant pursuit of applicable knowledge. To thrive, we must be growing in knowledge and wisdom at the same astronomical rate of today's technological advancement. We must make it our business to know what was, what is and what is to come. We must realize that knowledge is not just power, but more so an acute imperative to those who wish to survive and thrive in the world today. Gone are the days when "I don't know" may be considered humility. With the technological advancement and the network and net worth that are available in the world today, "I don't know" could easily depict stupidity, especially if you have not done the due diligence to know before being asked.

The more I read about other people's approach to life, their experiences and the experiences of other people that were graciously shared in print for the betterment of the world, the more I refined my own approach in order to avoid their mistakes. If you think the world seems to always be making the same mistakes, just imagine if history was not written down at all. You may have heard people say, "A stitch in time saves nine", but I have learnt that a book in time saves lives; that is, both the lives of the writers and the lives of the readers. Books have saved my life in many instances, as well as the lives of those who have attested to the benefits of curiously seeking knowledge in self-help books. If you read a good book about how to manage your anger and begin to relentlessly practice the principles therein, you may end up saving yourself from a situation where your anger may have caused a fatality.

Many of the things that I discovered about myself in the self-discovery phase of my journey en route to fulfillment made my purpose in life to become absolutely clear. Another thing that was made absolutely clear to me was how much I needed to learn, unlearn and relearn a number of life concepts. Basically, I had to be raised all over again; but this time, through Absolute Power. I had to embark on a quest to gain the wisdom, knowledge and understanding that is necessary to overcome the impact of a troubled upbringing. I had to become self-aware of my innate strengths and weaknesses; the propellers of my success and the deterrents of my fulfillment. I had to read other people's stories in order to be able to write my own. To sustain our journey en route to fulfillment, we must be seeking applicable knowledge consistently; always.

In a world where we are exposed to so much information and yet know so little, trying to acquire applicable knowledge could be very challenging; although, not as challenging as trying to apply it. It is easier to know than to do, easier to read than to practice. But my mind was made up–I was going to do whatever it took for me to live a life of purpose; and if the pursuit of knowledge, wisdom and understanding was an acute imperative in my journey en route to fulfillment, nothing was going to stand in my way. If I did not allow anything to stand in my way when I was living a life of self only, why should I allow something to stand in my way now that I am living a life of purpose?

Not leveraging these numerous sources of information and knowledge to support our journey en route to fulfillment is like allowing ourselves to starve in a blossoming garden of apples. If nothing else interests us, we should be learning about our purpose in life, about our Creator, about Creation. Of what use is it if we know everything and yet nothing about the God who created us, about our individual purpose in life? How much effort are you putting into the need to increase in knowledge, into the need to know, to understand, to grow, and to welcome greatness into your life? You may be loved without you having to do anything, but you cannot learn without you not having to do something. Everything may be offered freely but not learning. To learn, you must seek after it with due diligence and an unequivocal determination. You must have the openness and humility to accept it at every opportunity.

Not a lot of things are within our control in life; but the ability to know and grow is. It is within our control to learn from everyone and every situation, both good and bad situations. If we say "I don't know" about what we claim to matter, and do not make enough effort to find out, there is no excuse that would be able to bail us out. For we now live in a world where we are able to find enough information about whatever it is we claim to matter. To welcome greatness into your life, reading is not an option, but an acute imperative; and so is learning, practicing, seeking advice and praying.

Based on this realization, I bought a lot of books and attended a number of seminars and workshops. I also sought advice of spiritual mentors–an experienced mentor for each area of my life where I needed to grow the most. There was also a time that I checked myself in with a relationship counsellor to help me figure out how to deal with some of the deterrents of fulfillment in that area of my life. Every person I meet, I make an effort to learn from. I no longer allow race, religion or socio-economic status to determine who I hung out with. The more I grew in knowledge, the more God blessed me with wisdom. In due course, I started to gain understanding in many things that were initially foreign to me. As I grew in understanding, so did the number of people who came to seek advice from me. As the number of lives I got involved in grew, so did my knowledge and understanding about life itself. Learning is greatness.

If you wish to reengineer your mindset, to no longer be deeply troubled by the inconvenient truth, why are you waiting too long to devour the books that were written to help you and others with the same desire? If you wish to be more self-aware, to live a life of purpose, a life that counts for the betterment of the world, a life that would impact the world for generations to come, what are you waiting for to seek the wisdom of those who are talking the talk and walking the walk? What are you waiting for to extract nuggets of wisdom in the books that some sages graciously wrote before continuing their journey beyond this life? As King Solomon once said, "Desire without knowledge is not good". In fact, it is bad. To welcome greatness into your life, you must first build a pipeline of knowledge into your mind, a bridge of understanding into your heart, and a stream of wisdom into your soul.

I have learnt that to be reckoned with, to have the ability of navigating through the growing complexities of today's world, we must be consistently upgrading our thinking by tirelessly pursuing focused learning with ardour and attending to it with diligence. Pursuing the knowledge that stands to enhance our wisdom and understanding should be as necessary as eating and sleeping, as enticing as anything else that we never seem to get enough of. How sharpened are your tools for the tedious tasks that lay ahead of you? As I write this chapter, I am reading four books–one to enhance my leadership, two to enrich my spirituality and another to exhilarate my relationships. I have learnt that despite personal growth, there are still opportunities for more growth, for you cannot be growing without knowing.

In the initial stages of my journey, the primary focus was to build confidence in myself; confidence that I can live without cheating, succeed without lying, and love with no conditions. I needed to grow in the faith and confidence that are necessary to step out of my comfort zone. Inasmuch as it may seem basic, I had to learn how to think of others as much as I thought of myself. I had lived a life of self for so long that it was difficult for me to break that detrimental habit. I had to learn how to be open without prejudice, and how to be kind without expecting anything back. I had to learn more about what I needed to learn, unlearn and relearn, about my perceptions in life, leadership and love. I had to become a lover of knowledge, a servant of wisdom, and a fan of understanding. My hunger to know and grow had to supersede my hunger to eat and sleep. My desire to understand what life was all about had to supersede the fear of being ridicule and the shame of ignorance. What I needed to know, I made every effort to know. What I did not understand, I humbly asked of those who did.

Reading is the act of examining and grasping the meaning of written or printed characters, words, or sentences, while learning is the act, process, or experience of gaining knowledge or skill from what is being read. However, focused learning is an acute imperative to survive and thrive, the act, process, or experience of gaining specific knowledge or skill relating to a predetermined subject matter in life. Focused learning is when we purposefully seek the knowledge that is necessary to achieve a specific objective in life. It is this act of learning that prepares us to seize moments of greatness as they present themselves. In fact, our journey en route to fulfillment is all about learning, unlearning and relearning, it is all about practicing and growing.

To learn more about life matters, I read the Bible consistently. To learn more about leadership, I read most of John C. Maxwell's books; 'Thinking for a Change' was one of his books that really helped to shape my way of thinking, and so did James Allen's book, titled, 'As a Man Thinketh'. I am also a fan of Stephen Covey, one of the gurus of Personal Effectiveness. His book, titled, 'The 7 Habits of Highly Effective People' was a great help to me as well. To be a better man, Sam Laing's book titled, 'Mighty Men of God', introduced me to the great expectations God has of men. Two very helpful book titles, which I read to better understand how women often think are, 'A Life Worth Living' by Geri Laing, and 'A Woman's Worth', by Marianne Williamson.

To learn more about love, Marianne Williamson's books were instrumental. More than anyone I know, she has done a fabulous job in creating a cocktail of life and spirituality that helped me to overcome doubt, hurt, pain, hate, fear and shame, which are all renowned obstacles to love. Some of her titles that I found very helpful in my journey were, 'A Return to Love', 'The Gift of Change' and 'Everyday Grace'. I would not have come this far in my journey en route to fulfillment had I not been introduced to these books by other people. Which of your "friends" are helping you to grow in wisdom, knowledge and understanding? Every book I read increased my knowledge in the subject matter. And the more I grew in knowledge, the less I became nonchalant about crucial matters and arrogant in challenging situations; the more I was equipped and encouraged to maintain a forward momentum in my journey en route to fulfillment. The need to consistently increase your knowledge about life and whatever else you claim to matter cannot be overemphasized.

Ignorance is like a terminal illness which slowly eats away every opportunity to welcome greatness into your life. The financial stress that continues to destroy lives in our societies is more due to the lack of financial planning than it is to insufficient income. The marital stress which continues to destroy marriages in our societies is more due to the lack of wisdom, understanding and knowledge about what makes marriages work than the statistical claim of incompatibility. To deal with information overload, you must use spirituality to filter every piece of information that comes near your heart, mind and soul, and God will ensure that only what needs to enter you, enters. If you just keep your eyes on yourself without thinking of who may need to learn what it is you are learning, and you will be amazed at how much you grow.

If you are married, you should be reading books that teach proven techniques of how to maintain bliss in your marriage. If you are a parent with a strong desire to enhance your parenting skills, knowing fully well that this is one of the most challenging responsibilities in life, then you should be a regular customer at the self-help section in your local bookstores. Instead of wasting time in social media websites, you should be registered at websites that share applicable parenting techniques for raising children. If you want to grow spiritually, consistently dig deeper into the Bible, while pursuing corresponding explanations through other sources. It is easy to agree with these concepts but hard to do anything about it. But they are doable.

In the words of Alec Waugh, "There is so little time for the discovery of all that we want to know about things that really interest us that we cannot afford to waste it on things that are only of casual concern for us, or in which we are interested because other people have told us we ought to be". Whatever it is that is frustrating you in your journey en route to fulfillment has a solution; you just have to find it. The lack of career advancement and business growth has more to do with the fear of taking risks than the claim of limited opportunities. The decadence amongst our youth has more to do with failure on the part of their parents to apply the wisdom, knowledge and understanding which is necessary to raise awesome children in troubled times than the effect of violent video games.

What is it that you need to learn in order to achieve Enhanced Personality, Effective Leadership, Energized Marriage, Equipped Parenting, Enriched Spirituality, Enlivened Relationships, Exulting Health and Wellness, Empowered Career, Elating Finances, Exhilarating Business and an Exciting Life Purpose? What is the lethal information that was injected into your mindset at inception, which you must begin to unlearn, and perhaps, relearn? People say knowledge is power, but not if you don't know how to use it. Knowing how to do things does not mean we are able to do it. This is why knowing why and how to apply the knowledge we have is more powerful than knowledge itself.

I have benefitted from reading so much that whenever I open a book to read, I am filled with the excitement of a child who is attending school for the first time. I have experienced so much growth from what other people had to say that I am now open to what other people have to say. This does not mean that I read everything; in fact, it is not every book I buy that I read. It is not every book I start to read that I complete. And it is not every book I complete reading that I end up practicing. I make every effort to be open-minded, but not to the influx of junk into my sacred being; not to the information that would trouble my heart and the concepts that would disturb my soul. This is why you must first discover yourself before attempting to become self-aware; otherwise, what would you be self-aware of if you don't even know who you really are?

I am thankful that I finally know who I am, what I believe in, where I am going, and what I need to improve on in order to sustain my journey en route to fulfillment. I know exactly what I am pursuing in life and am strongly committed to "fighting the good fight, finishing the race and keeping the faith", as Apostle Paul puts it. To get you through the vast wealth of knowledge out there, you must know yourself. If it troubles your heart and disturbs your soul, then do not read it, watch it or even listen to it. If it challenges you to look into yourself, to know yourself and to grow in life, leadership and love, then you have likely stumbled upon wisdom in print. Read it. Devour it. Treasure it. Share it. I have learnt so much from sharing what I know, from being open to critics of what I so strongly believe in. I have learnt that regardless of how much we disagree with other people's opinion, there are often some nuggets of information therein that would either reinforce our own opinion or cause us to revaluate it.

Considering the chaos that the lack of love is creating all over the world, one topic we must consistently learn about is love. If we are going to ever welcome greatness into our lives, we must dedicate time to learn how to love one another, how to care for the planet, and how to live lives of impact. We must learn to prolong our lives through proper eating habits and exercising. We must learn to resolve conflicts completely, to manage our time effectively, and to make decisions that are beneficial to humanity. We must learn to "correct, rebuke and encourage with great patience and careful instruction", as advised by Apostle Paul. We must learn how to love and be loved.

To learn below one's capacity, or to stop learning altogether, is suicidal in every way–mentally, spiritually, emotionally, financially, socially and physically. This is because our refusal to learn slowly outdates our existing knowledge, wisdom and understanding. Our whole life, and often the lives of those whom we claim to love, will wither away by our refusal to learn. In retrospect, when we stop learning, we stop growing. And when we stop growing, we systematically begin the process of dying, slowly. Therefore, when we stop learning, we start dying. Whether we are growing or dying has more to do with our mental capabilities than our physical advancement. In our journey en route to fulfillment, we must consistently ask ourselves whether our physical growth is balanced or imbalanced with our mental capabilities.

To better determine where you should focus your learning, humbly ask your spouse, children, parents, boss, coworkers and friends, and they would gladly let you know. In most cases, it is not that we are unaware of what we need to learn, but rather, we do not make enough effort to begin the process. According to Sven Birkerts, "To open a book voluntarily is at some level to remark the insufficiency either of one's life or of one's orientation toward it. When we read we not only transplant ourselves to the place of the text, but we modify our natural angle of regard upon all things; we reposition the self in order to see differently. When we enter a novel, no matter what novel, we step into the whole world anew. For the space of our reading, and perhaps beyond, changes our relation to all things".

What are you waiting for to embark on your pursuit of the knowledge you need to welcome greatness into your life? Is it about dieting to control your weight and avoid high levels of cholesterols, which lead to heart disease? What are you doing to learn about household budgeting in order to avoid financial stress (currently the top reason for divorce in our societies)? Are you learning to see imperfect people, like you and me, so perfectly so that your love for yourself and others may steadily increase? A man who wishes to conquer the challenges of life must be a diligent seeker of knowledge. A man who desires to be respected by others must be willing to subject himself to wisdom. A man who longs for the understanding of life must make humble efforts to understand others without expecting to be understood.

I have learnt that greatness gravitates towards those who are in the constant pursuit of knowledge, wisdom and understanding; those who would passionately say, "Let me try", instead of saying "I can't"; those who would humbly say, "Let me get back to you", instead of saying "I don't know". If you are wise, your journey will be less challenging. If you are ignorant, you would have unfortunately compounded the challenges of life that lay ahead of you. Whether you choose to learn or not, you will; it just may not be what you should have learnt. Even King Solomon who is considered to be the wisest man to have ever lived is known to have always prayed to God for wisdom, to have passionately pursued knowledge through books, and to have humbly gained understanding through mentorship. He knew that he needed to gain these in order to rule his kingdom, in order to secure his position and fulfill his purpose in life.

If you are not wise in your finances, you will suffer. If you are not wise in your relationships, marriage and parenting, you will suffer. If you are not wise in your career and business, you will suffer. If you are not wise in your spirituality, you will suffer, both in this world, and in the world to come. Those around you will likely suffer as a result of your refusal to learn, but ultimately, you will suffer the most, with the added pain, guilt, fear and shame that your ignorance or stubbornness will be causing those around you. "I don't know" is a honourable thing to say until you do nothing about it; until you do not make enough effort to know. In your journey en route to fulfillment, you should always "be prepared to give an answer to everyone who asks you to give the reason for the hope that you have", as Apostle Peter puts it.

Contrary to popular notion, ignorance is not bliss. It is more like a disease that must be cured with the fierce urgency of now should you wish to welcome greatness into your life. As you start approaching life with the mindset to learn from every situation, humbly prepared to accept and work on whatever detrimental character traits of yours are brought to light, you will begin to position yourself for greatness. You will begin to grow mentally, emotionally and spiritually. You will begin to conquer challenges which once seemed insurmountable to you, and begin to blaze trails through areas that you never even knew existed. You will begin to welcome greatness into your life.

Almighty God,

You said through Prophet Hosea that people will perish for lack of knowledge. It is not that the world lacks knowledge, Lord, but rather the will to seek and accept it. And so Father, we thank you, first and foremost, for offering us the Book of Knowledge; for giving us the Bible that contains all the knowledge that is known to man. Thank you for offering us so much wisdom, knowledge and understanding.

What can we do with knowledge, Lord, without your guidance? How can we ever become wise without your blessing? What is understanding if not of you, Lord?

I pray Father that you instigate in me the desire to learn; the quest to start equipping myself with the knowledge that will save my life and the lives of those around me. Open my eyes to what I must read and my ears to what I must listen to. Open my heart, Lord, to the understanding of you.

May I become a great student of life, a humble man of knowledge. May I begin to seek you with all my heart and your message for me through every possible medium. May whatever knowledge we need to have about how to make ourselves and the world better be obvious to us, and may our hearts be softened enough to assimilate the knowledge of you.

Thank you, Lord, for always answering our prayers. As I continue to read this book, Please use the wisdom therein to help me draw closer to you, now and forevermore.

Amen.

Chapter 6

Rule of Engagement

> **"A man's growth is seen in the successive choirs of his friends".**
>
> **~Ralph Waldo Emerson**

In a world where there seems to be nothing wrong with being overly consumed with self, where many people and societies have become comfortable with things that lack integrity, and where some "friends" no longer deter each other from cheating on their taxes and spouses, why would anyone risk the possibility of reproach, ridicule and repercussion from "friends" to stand up for righteousness? In fact, how can any man be different from the people he hangs out with on a regular basis? One of the main reasons why I remained on the race of desires for so long was because I kept a company of likeminded people. To ease your transformation from selfishness to selflessness, from vanity to integrity, and from falsehood to authenticity, you must be ready to disengage yourself from the people you hang out with on a regular basis. You must be ready to disengage yourself from some of the people you call friends.

Due to the fear of reproach, ridicule and repercussion from family members and so-called friends, many people hold themselves back from making the necessary changes to welcome greatness into their lives. While we do not have the option of which family we are born into, we certainly reserve the right to choose our friends. A friend is someone who is attached to another by feelings of affection and personal regard; someone who cares for the personal and spiritual growth of another as much as his. Therefore, if any of your so-called friends would make jest of you or even attempt to discourage you from making the character changes that are necessary for you to welcome greatness into your life, that person is not your friend. This is why we must not be quick to confer this very delicate title of 'friend' on other people without very careful consideration of their ability to fulfill the associated obligations.

It was disheartening for me to realize that most of the people I called friends were neither attached to me by feelings of affection nor had personal regard for me. Despite the disappointment of knowing that literally none of them were willing or able to support me in the character changes that I needed to make, it was still hard for me to disengage myself from them because they were my childhood friends; they were people who shared great memories with me. This painful experience taught me that changes in personal principles and perceptions are like battles, for regardless of how tactful the changes are made, there will be casualties along the way. Even after coming this far in my journey en route to fulfillment, it will be naïve on my part to not expect more casualties in my friendships as I continually forge ahead.

If a smoker wishes to quit smoking, he should be ready to loose some of his associates who are unwilling to quit. If a wife wishes to selfishly abandon her marriage, she should be ready to loose some of her associates who are friends common to her and her husband. If you wish to become spiritual, then rest assured that your unspiritual friends will gradually desert you or you will have to eventually disengage yourself from them in order to sustain your spiritual journey. This is a key rule of engagement to sustain your journey en route to fulfillment; that is, if we claim to be heading in a certain direction in life, we cannot be in the midst of those who are heading the opposite direction.

A rule of engagement is a directive that is issued by a competent military authority, which delineates the limitations and circumstances under which forces will initiate and prosecute combat engagement with the other forces encountered. In military or police operations, the rule of engagement determines when, where, and how force shall be used. While the rules may be made public, as in a martial law or curfew situation, they are typically known only to the force that intends to use them. A very important rule of engagement in our journey en route to fulfillment is to diligently surround ourselves with true friends who are able and willing to help us to sustain the characters changes that are necessary for us to welcome greatness into our lives.

The journey en route to fulfillment is a major transformation; it is a paradigm shift that impacts not just your body, mind and soul, but also your associates and habits–who you hang out with, where you often go, what you often say, see, hear and feel must all be transformed in order to welcome greatness into your life. As Anatole France puts it, "All changes, even the most longed for, have their melancholy; for what we leave behind us is a part of ourselves. We must die to one life before we can enter another". Until you are ready to feel the pain, do not expect to feel the gain. Until you are willing to lose the fight, you are not ready to win the battle. To be self-aware, you must be aware of who the true friends amongst your friendships are. To know yourself better, you better know your friends better.

After very careful consideration, I came to the unwavering conclusion that everyone we associate with falls into one of the following six Categories of Friendship: Cheerleaders, Competent Advisers, Incompetent Advisers, Onlookers, Parasites and Impostors. This conclusion, which was born years ago out of the evaluation of my own group of associates, has been instrumental in helping many people to overcome their fear of being ridiculed by those they call "friends". Using this rule of engagement, I diligently examined my close associates to determine their ability and willingness to support my new way of being. The outcome was sad but eye-opening; it was painful but indisputable. Slowly but surely, the process of disengaging from some of them had to begin, with tact but unwavering assertiveness. It was unfortunate but very necessary.

True friends are not those who often sing our praises or dance to every tune of ours, they are not those who are often by our side or at our beck and call; but rather, our true friends are those who would always challenge us in our foolishness, rebuke us in our sinfulness, and exhort us in our laziness. Since a one-sided coin buys nothing in the marketplace, a true friend must be able and willing to balance encouragement with exhortation, laughter with cries, and cheers with rebukes. To welcome greatness into your life, you must never let the need to feel good supersede the need to be challenged, for therein lies the opportunities for personal growth.

Cheerleaders are those who lead spectators in cheering at a pep rally or athletic event. Often the second largest group amongst your associates after the Onlookers, they will sing your praises whether you are right or wrong, dance to every tune you play whether it is appropriate or not, and are at your beck and call even when it is unnecessary. Because of their biases towards you, they are not a group of people you should be seeking advice from. While you may want to keep a couple of them close by to cheer up people during celebratory events, it is unwise to rely on them for guidance and directions in your journey en route to fulfillment.

If you are a smoker who wishes to quit smoking, the Cheerleaders would cheer you on; and if you were to start smoking once again, they will cheer you on as well. They ignorantly believe that the purpose of friendship is strictly to make you happy, and therefore also expect you to cheer them on as well, even when they are going against the principles that are necessary to welcome greatness into their lives. If you surround yourself with too many of them, you will eventually become one of them as well–basically good for cheering and nothing else. According to King Solomon, "The one who has unreliable friends soon comes to ruin, but there is a friend who sticks closer than a brother." I had to disengage myself from those associates who seemed to care less about what the right things to do were and more about the need for me to always have my way in every situation.

Competent Advisers are those who would offer you their opinions and advices based on their knowledge and experiences in situations that are similar to yours. Often the second smallest group amongst your associates after the Impostors, a Competent Adviser would tell you what he did or experienced in a situation that is similar to yours without failing to point out the differences between your situation and his. Unlike the Cheerleaders who would cheer you on towards no direction in particular, a Competent Adviser will restrain himself from urging you towards any particular direction, while giving you information that should make you think deeply, act passionately and grow steadily. Whosoever wishes to be a Competent Adviser must walk consistently in the way of God and remarkably rely on the Holy Spirit for guidance and direction.

In addition to being worthy of respect and possessing vast knowledge and experience in specific areas of life, they are mature enough to be objective without being prejudicial, and know you well enough to have the understanding that is necessary for an advice to be effective. Competent Advisers are rare and often assume the roles of mentors to those who are humble enough to consider them likewise. To welcome greatness into your life, you must seek after them with ardour and listen to them with diligence. According to Alfred Lord Tennyson, “Knowledge comes, but wisdom lingers”.

Although generally known for their wisdom, Competent Advisers are sandwiched between Cheerleaders and Incompetent Advisers, which makes Cheerleaders and Incompetent Advisers often consider themselves to be Competent Advisers. Imagine a teenager asking another teenager for advice on sex, drugs and rock and roll. But then, this is what some adults do as well. They apply diligence when buying a home or when choosing a stockbroker for their investments but do not apply common sense when choosing who to advise them on crucial life matters. This is why it is very common nowadays for friends to lead each other astray. To be cheered up is sometimes necessary, but to be incompetently advised could be deadly. So be aware of the differences between these Categories of Friendship.

I have learnt that if the advice of a friend hardly pricks you, then that person is likely not a Competent Adviser. For while it may be uncomfortable for them as well, Competent Advisers will tell you the inconvenient truth even if it puts their friendship with you in jeopardy. Competent Advisers love you enough to challenge you when you are heading in the wrong direction, and care for you enough to offer up themselves as sacrifices if necessary to wake you up to your senses. How willing are you to challenge your friends on their lack of integrity? How comfortable are you to challenge your friends on their nonchalance, ignorance and arrogance? The reason that I couldn't challenge my associates back then was because I was likeminded. But since I began my journey en route to fulfillment, it has become easier for me to "correct, rebuke and encourage–with great patience and careful instruction", as advised by Apostle Paul, and I make every effort to do so with nothing but love.

Incompetent Advisers are those who believe they must have something to say about everything, even in areas where they have no knowledge and experience. While they may have your interest at heart, they are unqualified to advise you in most areas of life; although, they may have something to say in some cases. They would give you advice based on their own experiences, and quite often without having carefully considered the differences between your situation and theirs, and your abilities and theirs. Instead of urging you to seek help from professionals, they would hastily assume the positions of professionals with insufficient knowledge about the matter at hand.

It is wise to identify the Incompetent Advisers around you so you may be wary of their advice. After many futile attempts to tactfully disengage myself from some of the Incompetent Advisers in my life prior to my journey en route to fulfillment, I had to confront some of them directly. I remember telling one of them to desist from offering me advice even if I were to ask him for it. To help him realize his low level of competency, I gave him examples of how his advice would have complicated my situation. After that conversation, we dropped off each other's list of "friends", with no malice on my part. To sustain your journey en route to fulfillment, you must be willing to confront the Incompetent Advisers in your life. If anyone gives up friendship with you because you spoke the truth with love, he was likely an impostor.

In addition to the obvious gap in maturity between a Competent Adviser and an Incompetent Adviser, the first often offers unbiased feedback while the latter often offers biased feedback; the first often offers advice only when asked while the latter is quick to offer unsolicited advice. Which of your associates is quick to offer you words of advice, especially when unsolicited? Which of your associates seem to always give you advice that ends up complicating the issue at hand? Regardless of whoever is giving you advice, you must ensure that the advice is in line with certain spiritual principles before allowing them to come near your heart, mind and soul. It is better to not be advised than to be advised wrongfully, whether intentionally or unintentionally.

Onlookers are spectators, observers and witnesses who are always present when dramatic events unfold in your life, either out of obligation or mere curiosity. They would not do anything to warn or steer you away from impending calamities because they do not consider themselves friendly with you enough to do so; but yet, they always have a lot to say about what they saw and did not see whenever bad things happen. Onlookers are the largest group of people amongst your associates and they mingle themselves with Cheerleaders until adversity makes the distinction between both categories. Due to their proximity, your neighbours and coworkers would often fall into this category; therefore, seeking advice from them or expecting their support in the moment of trouble may be too high an expectation from them.

Often considered gossipers, Onlookers are quick to know when you are troubled because of their close proximity to you. And since they do not consider themselves friendly enough with you to "interfere", they would often line up behind the Cheerleaders without cheering you at all. While the Cheerleaders would cheer you on regardless of whether you are running the race of desires or marathon of life, the Onlookers would fix their eyes on you without expressing any emotion until you run out of their sight. Were you to stumble during your race, they would reposition themselves in order to watch whatever happens to you next so that they may broadcast the incident to everyone who cares to listen before the news hits the airwaves.

Parasites are those who live on your hospitality to receive support, advantage, or the like, without giving you any useful or proper return. They are like the organisms that live on or in another organism from the bodies of which they obtain nourishment. They are always around you and hard for anyone to get rid of them all. Whenever they show up to "help" you, it is mainly to get something back in return. Like a chameleon, they can alternate between other Categories of Friendship, while being deceitful enough to get whatever they want from you, without you even knowing it.

To support their parasitic nature, they will tell you what you would like to hear, when you would like to hear it, and how you would like to hear it. Their advices are strictly based on very careful attempts to not impact your hospitality towards them. While the Cheerleader may spur you on the wrong way based on your choice, they would often exhort you towards directions that would nurture your ego; towards directions that would make you swell with pride. According to Ben Elton, "The people who get through life dependent on other people's possessions are always the first to lecture you on how little possessions count". Parasites are able to make you feel good about the advices they offer you so that they may continue to feed off you as long as it takes for you to become wise enough to disengage from them.

Impostors are often the smallest group amongst your associates and the most dangerous pack of them all because their primary objective is to harm, hurt and destroy due to sheer wickedness or their jealousy or envy of you. It may also be to take revenge against you for something you or someone related to you may have done to them in the past, something you may likely not even remember! In the words of Jesus Christ, "They come to you in sheep's clothing, but inwardly they are ferocious wolves." Perfectly disguised as friends, Impostors do not mean well but yet, have deceitfully positioned themselves otherwise.

Impostors are so deceptive that they could easily alternate between the Categories of Friendship, while making every effort to position themselves as Competent Advisers until the day of reckoning exposes them as slanderers, gossipers, liars and betrayers. With the main objectives to derail and destroy, they would give nod of approval to every move you make and then criticize those same moves behind your back in such a way that you may blame others for their deceitfulness. An Impostor may be your friendliest neighbour, most supportive co-worker, and a well respected member of your church, but without a question, he or she is an axis of evil. They would play along with your decisions, but quick to say "I told you so", when trouble finally comes.

Impostors are diligent in their quest to destroy, resourceful in their desire to succeed (in their quest to destroy you), and conniving in their approach. Wickedness is their tool, deceit is their key, patience is their pride, and failure is not an option for them. They would set up your close associates in order to gain your trust and get closer to you. To earn your respect, they would hardly cheer you on like the Cheerleaders, barely give you any advice like the Competent and Incompetent Advisers, and scarcely feed off you like the Parasites. A perfect example of an Impostor is Judas Iscariot who worked and walked with Jesus Christ throughout His Ministry and then sold him for just 30 pieces of silver.

The rule of engagement made me become very aware of myself and those around me. It opened my eyes to how I had allowed other people to nurture my ego, how I had naively allowed other people to distract me from my purpose in life, and to keep me from beginning my journey en route to fulfillment. While I ended up learning it the hard way, like most people unfortunately would, the rule of engagement helped me to realize the enormous power friends have to either make or break you. When you call someone a friend, without having determined the category he or she falls into, you would be giving her the influence to directly or indirectly lead you astray from your purpose in life, and the ability to enable or disable monumental events in your life. Be nice to everyone but prudent about the ones that you allow to get closer to your heart. The process of building friendship is a very slow one and everyone must be tried and true before being allowed to assume this honourable role of a friend.

Before you go around labelling the people around you, you should first determine the category you fall into in every one of your relationships. How would you expect to be a true friend to someone else if you are not self-aware, if you lack a spiritual mindset, if you have not had a true friend yourself? In the words of Jesus Christ, "Do not judge, or you too will be judged. For in the same way you judge others, you will be judged, and with the measure you use, it will be measured to you. Why do you look at the speck of sawdust in your brother's eye and pay no attention to the plank in your own eye? How can you say to your brother, 'Let me take the speck out of your eye,' when all the time there is a plank in your own eye? You hypocrite, first take the plank out of your own eye, and then you will see clearly to remove the speck from your brother's eye." Being aware of who my true friends were helped me to become more aware of who I was, who I needed to be.

Are you an Onlooker in your workplace, church and community? How often do you get involved to resolve conflicts between other people? How often do you get involved with ongoing projects in your community or with the initiatives that stands to benefit the church you attend or the school your children attend? The rule of engagement demands that you offer a helping hand to someone you do not even know; that you participate in initiatives that may not benefit you; that you interfere when someone who you may not know well enough is heading the wrong direction in life. Regardless of what your purpose in life is, helping to inspire and guide the youth of today is a direct mandate from God to everyone.

While we may not want to see ourselves as Parasites or Impostors, it would be an outright lie to say that we have never assumed the position of an Incompetent Adviser with some of our associates. If you don't know what to say to an associate who is going through divorce, death of a loved one or depression, just let him know you will be praying for him, and then do so on a regular basis. Trying to offer someone else what you do not have or give advice without the necessary knowledge and experience has its roots in pride, arrogance and wickedness. We are not expected to always have something to say. In fact, sometimes, silence is golden. It is wise and humble to point people to others who likely have experienced whatever it is a friend is going through. You may also offer a book that provides him or her some guidance and suggestions.

When I was a child, my mother always warned me to be careful about my choice of friends, and to be even more careful when falling in love. Despite having been warned and well-advised, I still stubbornly had to learn these lessons the hard way. If husbands and wives were diligent enough to really know each other, rather than allowing themselves to be blinded by love, then the rate of divorce in today's societies would not be as high as it is. The people we choose as friends have the influence to encourage us when we are struggling, rebuke us when we are straying and challenge us when we are lazing. It is up to us to choose wisely or pay dearly.

Our true friends are those who are way more concerned about our integrity than our convenience, about our present than our past, about our future than our present, and about our soul than our body. When the time finally arrives to depart this world, if privileged enough to have one last minute of reflection, I would like to depart self-assured that I have been a true friend to many; that I said what needed to be said, did what needed to be done, and went where I needed to go in order to enable the journey of others, to make the world a better place, to make a difference in the lives of others.

One of the main reasons I have been able to come this far in my journey en route to fulfillment was because I finally disengaged myself from my associates who were heading the opposite direction from my purpose in life and then surrounded myself with likeminded people who are also determined about their journey en route to fulfillment. You cannot sustain the marathon of life in the midst of those running the race of desires, just as light and darkness cannot mix, nor can water and oil. Friendship is great, but not when it lacks absolute integrity, a shared vision, and mutual accountabilities. Friendship is a blessing that we must receive with caution, that we must be very grateful for and yet be very careful about.

Almighty God,

Thank you for creating the concept of friendship!
Thank you for recognizing how much we need to be encouraged by one another despite the powerful encouragement we could draw from your words.

I come before you this moment to ask that you help me to become a true friend to those around me.I pray, Lord, that you bless me with the wisdom and courage that is required to be a competent adviser to those around me. May I focus more on being a true friend to others than on others being a true friend to me.

I have been hurt in my lifetime by those I called friends. Help me Lord to be healed of whatever pain may have been caused me so that I am able to befriend others once again. May I be cautious about whomever I choose as friend, and be faithful to whoever befriends me.

Use me, Father; please use me to be a source of encouragement to my friends, to be an example of what you created the concept of friendship for. May I hold this honourable title dear to my heart and fulfill the associated responsibilities to the very best of my abilities.

Thank you, Lord, for being a true friend to us all! What a friend we have in you, Lord, for bearing all our sins on the Cross of Calvary. May we use you as a model of what a true friend should be!

Amen!

Chapter 7

Band of Encouragers

> **"We live by encouragement and we die without it – slowly, sadly and angrily."**
>
> **~ Celeste Holm**

While we would agree that we could use a regular dose of encouragement from the people around us, most people hardly receive any–and most likely, hardly give any either. And of course, we tend to blame this "oversight" on our busyness, lack of time, and forgetfulness; when in fact, many of us are simply just not making enough effort to encourage those around us. As a result of this "oversight", our spouse, boss, co-workers, neighbours, friends, family, children, parents and those we claim to love are only made aware of what they do wrong and barely anything they do right. This imbalance creates a strong feeling of discouragement, which is basically why many people no longer aim for the very best, but rather aim just to avoid the worst.

Since many of us no longer make conscious effort to encourage ourselves and those around us, encouragement is slowly becoming extinct in our workplaces and unpopular in our homes as well. And at this rate, it will soon become an archaic notion to the younger generation. In my journey en route to fulfillment, I have learnt that encouragement is the strongest form of love. I have learnt that it is what we need the most because everything we desire and do in life is based on our underlying need to feel encouraged. All the effort of man is usually based on the need to feel good and to look good. To sustain our journey en route to fulfillment, it is very helpful to find something or somebody to encourage us along the way; otherwise, the journey would be painstaking, tiresome and dull. Without a doubt, a much greater need than food and shelter is love. For love to be meaningful to anyone, it must be accompanied with a consistent dose of encouragement through words and actions.

Encouragement means to be inspired with courage, spirit, or confidence. It means to be promoted, advanced, or fostered by something or someone. Encouragement is inherent in who we are and what we do. It is yet another acute imperative in our journey en route to fulfillment. It is the fuel that is required for us to arrive at the ultimate destination. It is the essence of what we were born to do, what we were created for. It was not long into my journey that I realized the absolute need to be encouraging to others and to be encouraged by others as well. As soon as I realized the challenges that lay ahead of me on this road less travelled, I quickly formed a band of encouragers to spur me on in truth and love. I surrounded myself with cheerleaders and competent advisers to cheer me on and advise me respectively.

Despite the astounding richness and sophistication of nowadays, it is unfortunate to see how the world has gradually moved away from being encouraging (when there was less in it) to being discouraging (when there is more in it). And worse still is the fact that we are now rapidly moving from discouragement to depression at the same rate of technological advancement. If we were to spend a fraction of the billions of dollars profit from anti-depressant medication on strategies to ensure the inhabitants of earth encourage one another, there would be fewer cases of aggression, hate, murder, suicide, and even war and other large-scale catastrophic events and inhumane acts which our forefathers would have never conceived in their days. In retrospect, the root cause of the today's turmoil is the growing lack of encouragement.

When we go about our day with a conscious effort to encourage other people, instilling hope and confidence in them at every opportunity, stimulating and spurring them with courage and spirit during their challenging moments, they will in turn start doing the same for other people as well. If we care for the world so much and have intentions of helping to steer it away from hate towards love, and from chaos towards peace, we must immediately become an encourager to everyone else. We must become the voice of reason and the source of inspiration to everyone else. We must realize that we are the ones that we have been waiting for to make the world a better place for this generation and the next. Until we begin to embrace encouragement as an acute imperative to human survival, we would become extinct way before the worries of our planet colliding with a large meteorite ever materializes.

Considering the depressing news that the media bombards us with on a daily basis, why even bother sharing that "constructive criticism" with someone whom you barely take the time to encourage? Don't you know it is discouraging for anyone to always receive constructive feedback with no positive ones to buoy her level of confidence? Some researches have indicated that it could take up to five positive feedback for some people to be softened enough to welcome a constructive feedback without becoming defensive or discouraged. Encouragement is the ability to balance constructive and positive feedbacks in such a way that the recipient of the feedback is encouraged. I had to learn how to do this; I had to learn how to be conscious of the impact of feedback on both ends–whether the giver or receiver. Encouragement is a very powerful tool that we must be eager to use at every opportunity.

If you wish to sustain whatever it is you hold dear at heart–be it your leadership, marriage, parenting, spirituality, health and wellness, academics, finances and business–you must belong to a band of encouragers; people who believe in your objectives and are mature enough to offer you the encouragement that is necessary for you to keep pressing onwards. Pursuing the required knowledge to make things happen is an acute imperative, and preparing a plan to execute and sustain the goal is diligence; but having the right people around you to guide, support, encourage and motivate you all the way is wisdom. To welcome greatness into your life, you must belong to a band of encouragers; you must be a giver and seeker of encouragement. You must be willing to give plenty of it to others, way more than you expect to receive. Encouragement is the lifeline of joy, the vessel of fulfillment, and absolutely instrumental in your journey en route to fulfillment.

Whatever we do or say everyday has a direct correlation with how encouraged we are, and how encouraged the people around us would be. If we are not actively seeking to encourage other people, we would have likely become discouraging to them, and may even be partly responsible for the depression some of our friends are medicating themselves for. All it takes for us to help make this world a better place, to welcome greatness into our lives, is to express appreciation for the effort other people are making more than exposing their shortcomings. In fact, words of encouragement are known to help people grow enough confidence to overcome their shortcomings. The more encouragement we offer, the more we are encouraged. We cannot expect to be refreshed when we are known to be refreshing to no one.

We are often quick to identify those who seem to purposely seek encouragement, when, in fact, we should look no further than ourselves. Whether we see it this way or not, we are not different from each other. Our colour, choices and capabilities may differ, but not our innermost needs as human beings. Everyone craves encouragement regardless of the façade some of us may put up for others to see. If we are encouraged, we will shine, and if we are discouraged, we will not shine as much. That light from within is reflective of how encouraged we are. I have learnt that our true beauty would only be revealed when we feel encouraged, appreciated, supported, loved and cared for. Even more beautiful and powerful is the feeling derived from seeing the progress others are making in their journey because of the consistency of your encouragement.

Why not encourage your family and friends with a "Have a great day" on your way to work instead of choosing to be moody in the morning, because you desire more sleep than you inaccurately planned for? How could you justify walking straight to your desk upon arrival at work without wishing your coworkers "Good Morning", because of a project you have allowed yourself to be consumed by? What about the people you meet on your way, on the train, plane or in the elevator? Won't it make you feel good if they were to say "hello" to you with a smile? So why don't you initiate it without expecting them to reciprocate the next day? I have learnt that encouragement is mostly derived by giving it rather than by receiving it. Even though it literally cost nothing to encourage others, it is greatly appreciated by everyone. All it often takes is a smile, an uplifting remark, a friendly glance, a compliment, a gesture, a slight deviation from our natural occupation with self to the supernatural preoccupation with others.

The greatest opportunity we have to welcome greatness into our lives is the one we have on a daily basis to make people feel great. What people often regret the most towards the end of their sojourn on earth are the opportunities they missed to uplift others, to let people know how much they mattered, to make people feel the love they claimed to have for them. It will be regrettable to discover that we had allowed the busyness and challenges which we created for ourselves to overshadow our utmost duty of expressing love to people through the power of encouragement. According to William Arthur Ward, "Flatter me, and I may not believe you; criticize me, and I may not like you; ignore me, and I may not forgive you; encourage me, and I will not forget you; love me and I may be forced to love you."

How far behind would I have been in my journey en route to fulfillment were it not for my band of encouragers, people like Osagie Ihama, who is consistently candid in his approach and feedback, while making himself available to encourage through action. Other members of my band include Josie Martin and Adesuwa Ndulue, who, despite remarkable challenges of their own would always make the time to encourage me in words and action; Bola Ogunpolu, who many of us consider greatness in person, a Competent Adviser, and the humblest and most hospitable person that I know; Charles and Ogbitse Ezomo, for the encouragement and exhortation they have consistently offered me times without number. In fact, I am writing this chapter at a critical point in my life and only able to cope because of the steady encouragement of these great people who make up my band of encouragers. Through them, I have learnt that great people don't work for greatness, but rather they live for it; they don't aim to be great, but rather aim to make others great; they don't think of themselves as great, but yet, because of the consistency of their humility and good deeds, they would be considered nothing else by others.

I strongly recommend that you put down this book at this moment, write down your top five encouragers, and send them brief messages of encouragement through SMS, email or Social Media. Then follow up with a phone call within the next three days to reinforce your appreciation. Encouragement is the smallest but yet the most impacting way of enabling others to welcome greatness into their lives.

Are you fortunate enough to have true friends? Be one to them by encouraging them consistently, especially during their times of challenges. A true friend does not wait to be called upon for help; he knows when to offer assistance and does so consistently. While financial support is sometimes critical, encouragement, which is often the most beneficial emotional support we can give to anyone, is crucial for anyone to overcome anything. Are you privileged to be a manager or in some form of leadership? Never leave your place of work without having complimented those you lead, for the productivity that you desire so much is closely tied to how encouraged your workers feel. You and I know that life is not all about work, and that employees are often refreshed when their managers stop by their desk just to say "Hello" and ask about their families, rather than to discuss project updates. If you are to be self-aware of anything, let it be about the level of encouragement you give to others.

Are you blessed enough to have a spouse? Then make the exchange of encouragement a consistent habit in your relationship, for your marriage largely depends on how encouraged your partner feels. Ensure that you are each other's number one fan everywhere you find yourselves or someone else will assume that position to the detriment of your marriage. Are you blessed enough to have children? You must encourage them way more than you reprimand them. Your top parenting goal should be to make your home the place where your children feel loved and encouraged the most, to make your home a safe haven from the predators out there. As a parent, your topmost responsibility in life is to ensure that your family is consistently encouraged. Everything you do must be to accomplish this task.

Are you blessed enough for your parents to still be alive? Then never let them miss you! Hug them always! Send them words of affirmation, even if you do not think they parented you well enough. Without excusing their shortcomings, it helps to realize that our parents most likely did the best they knew how to in the circumstances they also found themselves in. And even if they acted out of arrogance or wickedness, we won't be able to welcome greatness into our lives until we forgive them, until we let go. As God commanded us through Moses, "Honour your father and your mother, so that your days may be long". This is the only commandment with a promise attached to it. If you wish to be forgiven for your shortcomings, you must be willing to forgive others as well, especially your parents. If you are not encouraging towards your parents, your children would most likely not be encouraging towards you too.

Be quick to contact people especially immediately after thinking about them. With the numerous ways of reaching people these days no matter where they are, what excuse do we really have for not being in touch with those we claim to love? After the sudden death of my brother many years ago, I learnt that life is like water in a boiling pot; from cold to hot may be gradual based on the level of heat that circumstances bring, but evaporation is imminent and often sudden. The death of my brother taught me to never ignore the nudges of the subconscious to contact and encourage someone because it may be the last opportunity that I have to do so before they pass on. I missed out on many opportunities to do so with my brother and now he is no more. To welcome greatness into your life, you must make every effort to encourage those you claim to love by not letting them miss you while you are still alive. Sometimes, all it takes to be encouraging to someone else is to just show up, and be present while there.

One of the most beneficial acts of encouragement is feedback. It is to be lovingly given some feedback on how to improve ourselves in certain areas of life. Inasmuch as everyone desires positive feedback, we would be missing out on very beneficial opportunities to grow if we disregard constructive feedback altogether. In fact, while positive feedbacks are great and should be offered freely to encourage people to maintain a forward momentum in their journey, the main key to becoming better at who we are and what we do is the constructive feedback we receive from others. This is why Ken Blanchard once referred to feedback as the breakfast of champions.

If you wish to welcome greatness into your life–whether in your personality, leadership, marriage, parenting, spirituality, relationships, health and wellness, academics, career, and finances, you must first be open to what others have to say about you, whether perceived to be truthful or not. You must be willing to humbly welcome constructive feedback as it comes, and even seek it out when it does not. You must be willing to suppress your natural tendency to be defensive or to retaliate. I have learnt that a man's strength lies not necessarily in his words, actions, power and might, but rather in his ability to humbly acknowledge his weaknesses and his determination to protect others from his shortcomings. How willing are you to find out what character changes you require to welcome greatness into your life? How open are you to what your friends have to say? Therein lay some unique form of encouragement that many people miss out on.

Whichever way we look at it, there is always an element of truth in the constructive feedback that we are graciously offered by other people even when it arouses in us high levels of pride and defensiveness. Rather than foolishly ignoring these nuggets of growth opportunity, ignorantly dismissing them as nonsensical, or arrogantly refuting them as if we are being attacked by an enemy, greatness demands that we humbly and diligently scrutinize them for the elements of truth regardless of how inconsequential we may consider those truths to be. It is not where you stand when everything is going well that really counts, but rather when you feel ignored, irritated or aggressed. It is how you react under these uncomfortable circumstances that determine who you truly are. The rate of your growth is directed related to how encouraged you are by the constructive feedback of others.

To welcome greatness into your life, you must be willing to embrace constructive feedback. How else do you expect to see your blind spot? How else do you expect to know things about yourself that irritates people the most? The need to be encouraged by positive feedback must never supersede the need to grow through constructive feedback. Both are absolute necessities. If you are always defensive towards constructive feedback, you would likely end up carrying the detrimental habit with you throughout your life. It is like hoping that a cancerous brain tumour would go away because we refuse to believe it is there. Every effort we make to defend ourselves against our own shortcomings is inadvertently spent trying to keep them. This is why the deterrents of fulfillment in our lives were created by our resistance to constructive feedback, our laziness to begin our journey en route to fulfillment.

Until we start seeing constructive feedback as encouragement, and are open to being 'criticized' by those around us, the maturity gap between our physical and mental states will gradually widen, thus making us way more mature in age than in wisdom. Until we start to humbly embrace the elements of truth which are embedded in what people sincerely think of us, willing to face ourselves, tackle our giants, and assume responsibility for our action and inaction, our mental, emotional and spiritual growth will be stagnated. To examine our lives goes beyond sitting still and thinking of it; it requires the opinions of those who see us the most, which is why feedback is a gift.

To welcome greatness into your life requires more action than words, more humility than sublimity. According to M. Scott Peck, "The tendency to avoid challenge is so omnipresent in human beings that it can properly be considered a characteristic of human nature. But calling it natural does not mean it is essential or beneficial or unchangeable behaviour. It is also natural to defecate in our pants and never brush our teeth. Yet we teach ourselves to do the unnatural until the unnatural becomes second nature. Indeed, all self-discipline might be defined as teaching ourselves to do the unnatural. Another characteristic of human nature–perhaps the one that makes us most human–is our capacity to do the unnatural, to transcend and hence transform our own nature." In essence, our lives do not really begin to count until what others think of us begins to count in our lives.

Although intangible, sincere feedback remains one of the most precious gifts that we can truly give to someone and also should wish to receive from those around us. It is so precious that only those who really appreciate us and our efforts would take the time to share their feedback with us. Accept it. Give it. Treasure it. I have learnt that to be alive is a gift from God, while to truly live is a gift to ourselves based on the choices we make every day. When we are no longer pricked by our consciences, saying and doing what we want, when and how we want things said and done without considering the impact on others, we would have regrettably given up our right to truly live. To welcome greatness into our lives, we must exude humility, gratitude and integrity in such remarkable ways that when we eventually pass away, our death will call others higher. If we are encouraging to no one, we would never be able to welcome greatness into our lives.

There are three main sources of encouragement in life: Self, Others and God. While we should surround ourselves with competent advisers and a few cheerleaders to spur us on, we must never forget to find ways to encourage ourselves as well. It is one thing to believe in yourself, and quite another thing to be self-encouraging. We have to use the positive feedback we receive to make ourselves feel good without swelling up with pride. If positive feedback is not forthcoming from those around you, then find one for yourself based on your accomplishment in life, and then celebrate it with friends or by yourself. Always find something to be grateful for, something to pat yourself on the back for, so that you are consistently encouraged.

Whoever said there was anything wrong with celebrating a milestone all by yourself? To encourage myself, I became comfortable with taking myself out to a movie or for dinner in a fancy restaurant whenever the right group of friends are unavailable. Those who find something wrong with self-encouragement often wallow in loneliness or end up either in the wrong crowd or in the wrong place. If I look back at the wrong places that I frequented in my days of rebellion, it was because I did not want to go to the right places alone, because I did not want to be considered weird by the people who saw everything wrong with taking yourself out on a date with yourself. I have learnt that we can only be self-motivating if we are self-encouraging, for encouragement always comes before motivation. Without encouragement, you will not be motivated.

If you are not making the necessary effort to encourage yourself, there is nothing anyone can really do to encourage you. If you are not being encouraged by others, it will be more challenging to welcome greatness into your life. If you are not drawing encouragement from God through His Words and prayers, you will be unable to live your life to the fullest. This revelation helped me to put things into perspective, for I now realize that whenever I am struggling to achieve anything in my life, it is likely because I am not drawing enough encouragement from these three main sources. We have the encouragement that is required for us to welcome greatness into our lives if we would only be humble enough to draw encouragement from God through His Words and prayers, and from ourselves through the little things we accomplish.

Give someone a hand, and he may walk a mile with you. Offer him some words of encouragement, and he will carry your words in his heart forever. As energy is vital to the body, so is encouragement to the soul. Those who withhold encouragement from others will never be encouraged. Regardless of how empty, confused or broken a man may be, he will eventually overcome his challenges with just a steady flow of encouragement from those around him. Regardless of the reason people claim to have committed suicide, it is ultimately because they lack the encouragement to carry on with life. The people who have gone far in life today will tell you that they went far because someone else always encouraged them. Who is going further in life today because of your words of encouragement?

Despite the magnitude of our challenges and the discomfort of our situations, the question is never whether we can overcome, whether we can achieve and conquer; but rather the question is if we believe we can, if we are willing to put in what it takes to achieve and conquer, if we are patient enough for the outcome to eventually be successful. Instead of complaining, we must be adamant about succeeding. Instead of procrastinating, we must be persistent in our efforts to succeed. Instead of quitting, we must continually set a new standard of patience and excellence. Before we label anyone as difficult, we should always ask ourselves if we have been encouraging enough for them to start making the necessary effort to grow and blossom. All it takes for people to open the floodgate of their hearts is for us to open the window of ours. If we have not poured out our heart to someone, it is arrogant to point our finger at the person.

Inasmuch as we tend to admire other people more than ourselves, we can only appreciate beauty because of the beauty that exists within us. Regardless of the dazzling beauty of our outward being, it is still incomparable to the beautiful intricacies of our inner being. A garden of the most beautiful flowers on earth is yet to compare with the beauty that exists within us, whether we feel encouraged or not. Whatever beauty stuns you the most today remarkably pales in comparison to the beauty you will discover about yourself tomorrow. The journey en route to fulfillment may look bleak, but so does every route to success.

Almighty God,

Thank you for the encouragement you provide to us every day through your creation.

Thank you for the encouragement you provide to us every day through the blessings that you continue to shower upon us.

Thank you, Lord, for giving us enough to be encouraging about, enough to be encouraged by – even though we are sometimes oblivious to these facts.

May we recognize and seize opportunities to be encouraged and be encouraging every day. May we be appreciative of the encouragement we get without being critical, hardened or timid. May we imitate the biblical Joseph of Cyprus, whom the apostle called "son of encouragement" so that those around us are consistently encouraged by the words of our mouth and by the works of our hands.

Forgive us, Lord, for even allowing discouragement to creep into our lives, for allowing Satan to have a foothold in our hearts due to our ingratitude and laziness.

Help us to continue to make the effort that is necessary to bring honour and glory to you by how encouraging we are to others by our actions, by how encouraged we are because of your love.

We pray this through our LORD, Jesus Christ,

Amen.

Chapter 8

Outbreak

"The tendency to whining and complaining may be taken as the surest symptom of little souls and inferior intellects".

~ Lord Jeffrey

One of the unproductive things human beings are known for is to complain. It is to quickly identify where the doers of deeds could have done things better. It is to quickly identify what is wrong with everyone around us, and with everything that everyone else does. Rather than applauding the positives and commending the efforts that people make, we are often quick to complain about what is not working well in machines, processes, policies, events, systems, and people, while saying nothing about what is working well. To welcome greatness into our lives, we must refrain from complaining, desist from blaming others, and resist the temptations to make excuses for our shortcomings. Animals must be taken aback at how much human beings complain despite the remarkable advantages and benefits that we have over them.

It was in a recent vacation to the Dominican Republic that I was heartily reminded of the humbling effect of poverty; about how poverty can prompt us to become very grateful for whatever life has to offer. Due to our insatiable nature, the more we have, the more we complain. Conversely, the less we have, the less we complain and the more we appreciate whatever we have. This maxim seemed even more pronounced to me because the tourists with whom I took a three-hour bus ride from the resort to the international airport complained all the way about one thing or the other. With focus on themselves and what they got and didn't get, they used vicious words to tear down the experiences that some of us were appreciative for. What an irony it is that we are of the richest generation ever and yet also of the worst complainers ever. As James Allen once said, "The very fact that you are a complainer shows that you deserve your lot".

Without mentioning anything about the sun, sea and sand that brought us thousands of kilometres away from our countries of residence to this beautiful island, or the tan that some tourists would be boasting about upon arrival in their G7 nations, or the luxury that a lower currency value afforded us in such a beautiful island, they ceaselessly complained about the resort, food, drinks, cleanliness, bus ride, bus driver, local people–and the list goes on and on for as long as the three-hour journey lasted! There was not one single word of gratitude to God for His travelling mercies, for keeping us safe and healthy during our memorable vacation. They had nothing nice to say about the men and women who slaved to make us comfortable during this memorable vacation. It is unfortunate to see people who are so privileged and yet so unappreciative, so fortunate and yet so nonchalant, arrogant or ignorant.

According to Theodore Roosevelt, "It is not the critic who counts; not the man who points out how the strong man stumbles, or where the doer of deeds could have done better. The credit belongs to the man who is actually in the arena, whose face is marred by dust and sweat and blood, who strives valiantly; who errs and comes short again and again; because there is not effort without error and shortcomings; but who does actually strive to do the deed; who knows the great enthusiasm, the great devotion, who spends himself in a worthy cause, who at the best knows in the end the triumph of high achievement and who at the worst, if he fails, at least he fails while daring greatly; and his place shall never be with those cold and timid souls who know neither victory nor defeat." To sustain our journey en route to fulfillment, it is absolutely crucial that we should not be the critic, but rather be the one "whose face is marred by dust and sweat and blood, the one who strives valiantly."

The tourist who started it all even had the prideful audacity to incite others against returning to neither the resort nor the country. Were I not self-aware enough and carefully observant of the situation, I may have been infected by this outbreak of complaints as well. Having travelled away from home hundreds of times in my lifetime, I have definitely stayed at hotels and resorts which I would rather not return to were I to revisit the same city or country; however, this particular resort at the Dominican Republic was far from it. It was decent, and the staffs were very friendly, dedicated and entertaining. In the words of Julia Moss Seton, "We have no more right to put our discordant states of mind into the lives of those around us and rob them of their sunshine and brightness than we have to enter their houses and steal their silverware". How appreciative are you of the places you vacationed? How appreciative are you of the people who serve you on a daily basis–in the coffee shop, restaurant, bookstore, bus driver, and etcetera? How appreciative are you for what you are, what you have?

If you are of the opinion that everyone is entitled to their opinion, it is very important for you to realize the major differences between destructive and constructive feedback. A destructive feedback is void of love and riddled with malicious intentions to disprove, discredit, damage and destroy, while a constructive feedback is offered with the intention of helping to improve and promote advancement. A destructive feedback causes injury, while a constructive feedback is meant to bring about healing. A destructive feedback is beneficial to no one–neither the giver nor the receiver, while a constructive feedback is beneficial to the receiver, whether they appreciate it or not. Which type of feedback do you often give to other people? Which type of feedback would you like to receive? Then ensure you give the same to others as well.

In the early stages of my journey, I had to learn how to tactfully offer constructive feedback to other people. Just as much as I expected others to accept my feedback with humility, I had to work on developing humility for me to accept theirs as well. To welcome greatness into our lives, our words must be seasoned with grace, truth, love and a remarkable desire to encourage improvement in people, things and situations. On the contrary, a rampage of destructive feedback benefits no one and will gradually damage our relationships, derail our journey and then eventually destroy us. Until we begin to pronounce the good in other people, other people will denounce us for our shortcomings. This is why we must be immunized against this contagious outbreak.

The issue that some of us have with constructive feedback is not often with the voicing of opinions but rather with the unfair judgment, harsh words, disrespectful attitude and arrogance with which the opinions are delivered. If we are honest with ourselves, we would agree that we have offered destructive feedback to others many a time. At one point or the other, we have offered feedback to one person or the other without the due respect, and without the honourable intention of offering them the necessary help to overcome whatever we see them struggling with.

A number of people blame the youth for one thing or the other and yet are not willing to mentor one of the youth they blame. These people complain about youth-related violence and yet have never contributed a dollar to youth camps and other youth development initiatives in their neighbourhood. If we were to ask the tourists on that bus during my trip to the Dominican Republic, we would likely discover that they did not take the time to complete the feedback form provided at the resort, and yet complained all the way disrespectfully. I have learnt that those who often complain about others are those who have not contributed anything towards the happiness of those they are complaining about. To welcome greatness into our lives, we must give up the right to complain even in the situations where we have been truly offended.

The world has seen numerous outbreaks in recorded history, with some of the most devastating ones of our era being polio, cholera, yellow fever, malaria, Ebola, syphilis, SARS, tuberculosis, swine flu, smallpox, chickenpox and now AIDS. But while these have been contained to commendable degrees, the outbreak of complaining about everything, blaming everyone else and excusing ourselves in every situation remains unchecked and uncontained, thus making it to spread like wildfire. Every where we go these days, we will find people complaining about something without willing to do anything about what they are complaining about.

An outbreak is a sudden, violent or spontaneous occurrence of disease or strife. It is an outburst, eruption, insurrection, revolt or mutiny of something that has been waiting to happen. It is often used to describe surprising and unexpected diseases that break out in specific regions. An outbreak creates chaos, and if uncontained, quickly becomes a pandemic, a global disease outbreak. This is what the combination of complaining, blaming and excusing is fast becoming–a pandemic. They are infectious character diseases which continue to derail many people in their journey en route to fulfillment and to hinder them from welcoming greatness into their lives.

The infected are quick to blame the weather or traffic whenever they are late for appointments even though they could have begun the journey earlier enough to arrive on time. They blame the government and police for the violence in their communities and yet do nothing to encourage those at risk. They blame their bosses for their lack of professional development, blame their detrimental character traits on their parents and blame their spouses, children and church leaders for their lack of personal and spiritual growth, but yet prefer TV programs, sports and working overtime to fellowshipping with spiritually-minded people. They complain about so many troubles in their lives, and yet hardly consult with their Maker through prayers, barely fellowship with others to get encouragement, and never confess their sins for healing purposes.

They complain about their weight and then complain about the effort required to loose it. They pray to have a job and then complain about their job description. They complain about a busy week and then complain that a long weekend was too short. They never adhere to the budget they prepared for themselves and then complain of financial difficulties. They pray to get married and then complain about their spouse. They pray to have children and then blame the children for tiring days and sleepless nights. Some women blame the men who got them pregnant while some men actually turn around to blame the women whom they impregnated! Does it no longer take two to tango?

As a people, we have become too focused on our entitlements, on our societal rights and privileges. We have become a people that disregard our responsibilities on purpose because it is easier to blame others for our mess. We have become a people who expect everyone else to fulfill their obligations but ourselves; a people who expect so much from others and nothing from ourselves. In my journey en route to fulfillment, I have learnt that it is only the ungrateful minds that complain. I have learnt that if we take our eyesight for granted, we will be blinded by our egos. If we are unwilling to do something about whatever it is we are complaining about, we may as well turn our complaints into praise.

As a country, we promote unnatural schemes like gay marriages, abortion, and euthanasia, in direct contradiction to God's plans of reproduction, and then complain about low birth rates and a declining population. We do nothing to discourage impure sexual activities like prostitution and homosexuality, and then complain about the increasing cases of HIV in our societies. We legalize tobacco and marijuana, and then complain of the increasing cases of smoking-related diseases and deaths. As a society, we have reduced the 'legal' age of having sex to barely that of a teenager, and then complain about increasing teen pregnancies. It is unfortunate to see how the self-destructive act of complaining has now become part of the DNA of many people.

We tell our teenagers that they are not mature enough to vote until a certain age, but yet okay for them to have sex way before that age. We ban prayers and the teaching of basic morals from schools, and then complain about the escalating violence amongst our youths. Sadder still are instances where some of us in authority have also turned around to blame the people we are meant to lead: Parents are blaming the children they are meant to raise in the way of the Lord; bosses are blaming the staff they are meant to motivate; and church leaders are blaming the congregation they are meant to inspire. The world is not progressing as much as it could because many of us have become very comfortable in the back seat of an immobile vehicle rather than helping to drive the change to make the world a better place than when we first came into it.

The acts of ignorantly complaining, arrogantly blaming others, and nonchalantly making excuses are as infectious as any outbreak of disease. It takes one person to complain about a train that is late and most people on the platform will get infected and complain as well. The immunization against this outbreak of complaining, blaming others and excuse-making is overflowing gratitude, unconditional compassion and absolute humility, respectively. It is to be self-aware and carefully observant of what is going on around us at every given time. Until we are grateful for whatever we receive regardless of how insufficient, we are vulnerable to this outbreak. Until we are compassionate towards the shortcomings of other people regardless of the impact, and humble enough to acknowledge our shortcoming regardless of the validity of "excuses", we would be unable to welcome greatness into our lives.

While our rate of complaints is directly related to our level of gratitude, our rate of blaming other people and making excuses is directly related to our levels of humility and compassion. The more we complain, the more we blame other people and the more we make excuses. The more we blame other people, the more we make excuses, and the more we complain. When we complain, we are directly laying blame and indirectly excusing ourselves. The people who have become experts in making excuses are experts at nothing else. We may make lots of effort and yet still fall short of our expectations, but when we begin to blame others for our shortcoming, we have given up the right to achieve or sustain whatever it is we are pursuing.

When we complain about other people, we are basically saying that we are way better than they could ever be, and that we would undoubtedly outperform them in their jobs despite Apostle Paul's advice to "consider others better than ourselves, in all humility". When we complain of authorities, we are saying that they are not of God's, even though the Bible commands us to "submit to the governing authorities, for there is no authority except that which God has established". When we complain about our marriages, we are saying that despite God's desire for "a man to leave his father and mother and be united to his wife, and they will become one flesh", we can never be united and become one flesh with our spouse because of the challenges which are notably common to marriage.

Rights and privileges are among the greatest blessings from God, for after creating the world, God gave us the ultimate right and privilege to "be fruitful and increase in number; fill the earth and subdue it. Rule over the fish of the sea and the birds of the air and over every living creature that moves on the ground." However, the abounding rights, privileges and paramount affluence in some societies have caused many people to become prideful enough to create exclusive clubs for themselves while a way larger portion of the world's population continuously struggle to have just enough to remain alive amidst perpetual famine, recurring ethnic cleansing, unending civil and tribal wars, extremely oppressive governments, mass tortures, and excruciating poverty.

What have you complained about this week and what are you doing to make things better? Who have you blamed this week, and what are you doing to avoid a recurrence of the situation? How many excuses do you find yourself making on a daily basis and how many of these situations could you have made enough effort to avoid? Blaming other people for our negative feelings and counterproductive actions are the immature attitudes that separate children from adults. While we may have been victimized spectators in the unfortunate circumstances of our childhood, we are now major players in whatever circumstances we find ourselves as adults, whether fortunate or not. In our journey en route to fulfillment, we no longer have the luxury to complain without doing anything about it.

To welcome greatness into your life, you must stop complaining and start appreciating. You must stop blaming others and start being compassionate. You must stop making excuses and start embracing humility. Make every effort to be diligent, and to follow through with all your promises. Always evaluate yourself, and humbly accept responsibility for whatever you could have done to make things better, whether it was your responsibility or not. Since we are unable to change other people, focus on controlling yourself and emotions, changing your attitudes and perspectives with the hope that others may be inspired and influenced by your determination, effort and consistency. When we channel the energy we spend complaining into encouraging others, the world would be friendlier, humbler and more productive.

When we start focusing on ourselves in every situation rather than pointing fingers at others, humbly seeking the life lessons in all circumstances rather than arrogantly pointing a finger at those who may have faltered, then our frustrations in life and business will gradually dwindle away. When we start the challenging journey of returning back to love rather than looking for someone to blame for the hate in the world, we would have positioned ourselves for peace that transcend human understanding. When we start making every effort to find our way back to God from the hole we dug for ourselves rather than looking for someone to blame for pushing us into the hole, we would begin to welcome greatness into our lives. To be self-aware is to know, accept and be watchful for whatever it is we are self-aware of.

To sustain your journey en route to fulfillment, you must beware of the outbreak and be immunized against it. You must protect your heart from arrogance, your mind from ignorance, and your soul from nonchalance. Most people are often shocked at where they find themselves in life when all the while they were heading that direction. It is only when we immunize ourselves against this prevailing outbreak would we be able to run the Marathon of Life, Leverage Absolute Power, build a Band of Encouragers, and Return to Love. It is only when we claim full responsibility for our thoughts, decisions, actions, inactions and reactions would we be able to welcome greatness into our lives and businesses. Then and only then would we become peaceful and peaceable, sincere and serene.

Almighty God,

You are to be praised from generation to generation. Words and actions are insufficient to express the honour and glory that are due you. When we consider all that you have done to meet even the needs we have not yet determined in our journey en route fulfillment, we are deeply humbled and in awe of your care and compassion.

I come before you humbled by your patience, guidance and protection. I acknowledge my ingratitude in areas of my life that I have been oblivious to your blessings. I confess being ungrateful in (name three areas that you complain about the most) I confess, Lord, the urgent need to stop complaining, stop blaming others and stop making excuses.

Thank you for your never ending provision for me, your never ending protection of my life. Thank you, Lord, for being kind enough to listen to my prayers this very moment, For always willing to forgive, support and guide me in my journey en route fulfillment.

Help me to humbly identify and tirelessly tackle the deterrents of fulfillment on my path. Help me to guard my heart against temptation, to stretch my mind to higher levels of wisdom, to exude my strength in every challenge, and to remain on this journey en route to fulfillment forever and ever.

Amen.

Chapter 9

Empty Vessel

"Man was born free, but everywhere he is in chains".

~ Jean Jacques Rousseau

We live in a world where wars are raging, diseases are spreading, wealth is hoarded, resources are scarce and morals are decaying. We live in a world where poverty is rampant, children are abused, integrity is disregarded, loneliness is prevalent and enthusiasm is extinguished. These unfortunate things are happening in the world because many capable people are afraid to act, to confront, to speak up, to stand up, to take risks, to grow. Due to the fear of possible reproach, ridicule and repercussion, many capable people in the world choose to do nothing about everything, and thus limit the scope of their own lives while watching others make the same mistake too.

The mere thought of beginning my journey en route to fulfillment was scary to me. Besides the fear of not being able to complete the journey, there was the fear of loosing friends, of being perceived as a weakling, of being mocked by my associates, of being called a church boy or some of those names that seem to scare some of us. Out of all the fears I had, my greatest fear was that of not being able to sustain the changes that I needed to make. I had seen people quit smoking only to return back to it in no time. I had seen people begin the journey of loosing body weight only to have it increased in time for the next round of New Year Resolution. Out of all my fears, therefore, the topmost was the fear of failing backwards. I was scared of returning back to my vomit, afraid of going back into the mud after having being washed so clean by the electrifying Blood of Jesus, the inestimable Grace of God.

Fear is a distressing emotion that is aroused by impending danger, evil or pain, whether the threat is real or imagined. It is the condition of uncomfortable uncertainty, a feeling that causes us to restrain ourselves from an action that stands to benefit us due to perceived failure or possible embarrassment. When we are afraid, our ability to act is inhibited regardless of whatever may be at stake. Fear is the main reason why many people no longer aim for the best, but rather aim just to avoid the worst. It is the reason why many people are yet to begin their journey en route to fulfillment. It is the reason why many people are living lives of emptiness in a world of plentiful.

Are you one of those who often allow the fear of failure to keep you away from acting; to keep you from taking control of your life, from stepping up, from reaching for the stars, from making a positive difference in your sphere, from beginning your journey en route to fulfillment? Are you one of those who would rather do nothing in order to avoid the criticism that might follow possible setback? Are you one of those who, for fear of what people might say, walk away from someone you love, someone who loves you? Are you one of those who avoid the inconvenient truth by refusing to either examine your conscience or accept the unfortunate events of your upbringing?

Are you one of those who, for the fear of confrontation, chooses to not initiate peace even when war is brewing, to not instigate change even when it is overdue, to not ask even when you do not know, to not speak up even when the lives of others are in danger, and to not inspire others even when it is much needed? Are you one of those who, for the fear of rejection, withhold the love you must give; for the fear of being considered weak, avenges a wrong that was done to you; for the fear of being unable to explain the reasons for your belief, hides your faith in God from other people? You are either going to be held back by fear or be motivated by faith.

Despite the ability to disguise itself as a 'less severe' hindrance of greatness, fear is the most serious obstacle to success in everything we do. It has, and continues to paralyze lives and jade dreams. It continues to deter the progress and accomplishments of many people. It continues to hold people back from becoming who they were created to be. Due to the fear of failure, of being ridiculed, challenged and persecuted, capable people regrettably restrain themselves from honourable opportunities to make a difference in the world. Like Edmund Burke once said, "The only thing necessary for the triumph of evil is for good people to do nothing". What is the evil that is triumphing today because fear is holding you back from doing something about it?

Before blaming people and circumstances for our situations, we must ensure that our roadblock of fear is completely demolished– be it fear of failure, oppression or opposition. Before we point an accusing finger at those who did nothing to prevent slavery, the massacre of six million Jews in Europe or the tribal war that eliminated about one million Tutsis in Rwanda, we must ensure that we are among the few who are known to speak up, to write up and to act up about things that should not be. Whether we are held back by fear or not, life is a succession of risks; so we may as well learn to take risk or be willing to die from avoiding it. What are you doing today to eliminate whatever fears are holding you back from welcoming greatness into your life?

Like the words of someone with no integrity, fear is just an empty vessel that unfortunate life experiences has docked in the lives of many people, limiting their greatness by creating perceptions of potential failure in whatever noble tasks they have at hand. Even when fear is valid, it is still made up of nothing; it is still an empty vessel. To be empty means to be void of any substance; to contain nothing or none of the usual or appropriate contents. It means to be destitute of quality; to be without force, effect, or significance. It means to be hollow, meaningless, and to lack purpose. This is what fear is. Nothing!

In order to overcome fear that may be as intimidating as Goliath was, you must confront it like David did. Until you are bold enough to preparedly, prayerfully and persistently confront your fears, they will hinder you from welcoming greatness into your life, from embarking on your journey en route to fulfillment. It held me down for many years, for those later years of my rebellion were regrettably prolonged by my fear to embark on my journey en route to fulfillment. Besides the fear of failure, I was also scared of what I may discover in the baggage of my childhood, pains that I did not want to remember and hurts that I did not want to deal with.

To overcome my fears, I had to act against them with passion. To conquer them, I had to fight against them with courage. Along the way, I learnt that the only person who can truly stop me from becoming the achiever I was created to be is me. The only person who can truly stop me from reaching the pinnacle of my existence is me. The only person who can derail me from my journey en route to fulfillment is me. In essence, fear is illusionary, a perception that benefits no one. What truly hinders us from welcoming greatness into our lives is not fear, but rather our unwillingness to confront it with everything we have.

While you may need the help of a life coach or other qualified professional, the only person who can help you to conquer your vessel of fear is you. The only person who can also fathom the fulfillment that awaits you upon conquering your vessel of fear is you. Perhaps the possibility of failure is holding you back from pursuing the academic qualifications you require to advance your career. Perhaps the fear of being considered vulnerable is holding you back from forgiving someone who may have hurt you a long time ago. Perhaps the fear of shame is holding you back from admitting a wrong that is now hindering your peace of mind. What are the fears that are holding you back today from welcoming greatness into your life, from embarking on the honourable journey to rid yourself of the impacts of unfortunate childhood experiences, the peace of mind that you so desperately desire?

To welcome greatness into our lives, we must be determined to triumph over our obstacles. We must be willing to be ridiculed for what is right. We must be willing to be considered different, difficult or delusional when standing up for humanity. We must be willing to say yes when others say no and to say no when others say yes, not just to be contrary, but to stand up for what is right. We must be willing to proclaim our values and stand by them even when they are unpopular. We must be willing to profess our faith even when other believers shy away from it. We must be willing to stick out our necks for the oppressed, stand up for the poor, and face any opposition to justice. This is how to overcome fear. This is welcoming greatness into our lives.

Doing nothing about the things we need to do something about is beneficial to no one. Allowing ourselves to be intimidated by fear keeps us away from the fulfillment we desperately seek in life and away from the impact we were created to make in this world. It was when I came to embrace Absolute Power that I realized that my fears were nothing but mere illusions. Even though a few of my fears has come to past since I began my journey en route to fulfillment, the benefits in every one of the situations turned out to remarkably outweigh the impact.

I have learnt that regardless of how monumental our fears may seem, we are definitely more powerful than we think we are. To embark on this discovery, we must confidently seize the opportunities that life presents us with to make a difference every day we are privileged to be alive, without succumbing to the empty vessel of fear. In the words of Apostle Paul, "In all things God works for the good of those who love him, who have been called according to his purpose."

One of the main reasons people fall short of their goals is that they do not ask for the help they require due to the fear of being turned down. Even when help is graciously offered, some people would turn it down for the fear of being considered incapable. Due to the fear of being mocked for an incomplete task, major undertakings like starting a new business, embarking on educational pursuits, or joining a weight-loss program are never started. What are the undertakings that you are shying away from because of fear? What are the situations that you are maintaining the status quo on because of fear? What are the opportunities that you are giving up because of fear? A very interesting thing about life is that we can have many of the same things in life, but life itself. We only have one life, and choosing to not maximize it due to some fears that may not come to pass, is the most regrettable thing we can ever do.

In the words of Marianne Williamson, "Our greatest fear is not that we are inadequate, but that we are powerful beyond measure. It is our light, not our darkness that frightens us. We ask ourselves, 'Who am I to be brilliant, gorgeous, handsome, talented and fabulous?' Actually, who are you not to be? You are a child of God. Your playing small does not serve the world. There is nothing enlightened about shrinking so that other people won't feel insecure around you. We were born to make manifest the glory of God within us. It is not just in some; it is in everyone. And, as we let our own light shine, we consciously give other people permission to do the same. As we are liberated from our fear, our presence automatically liberates others." It is no doubt that some of us are scared to begin our journey en route to fulfillment because of the fear of arriving at the destination. It was one of my fears too.

The most dangerous place we can ever find ourselves in life is at the crossroad of uncertainty. It is to stand still in one place for too long without knowing which direction to head in life because of fear. When we allow the fears of change, setback, mistake and ridicule to render us immobile, we will eventually get run over by those whose focus and determination are fuelled by strong desires to attain greatness. Come to think of it: Many people are stuck in life because they are afraid of being stuck! It is the fear of being seen as light, the fear of being looked up to for leadership and love that is making some people to no longer aim for the very best. It is as if they wish to be in the spotlight and yet, at the same time wish otherwise.

What we fear the most is nothing else other than the expectations of adulthood. We wish to be recognized as adults, but like children, we are scared of the accountabilities and responsibilities of adulthood. We are scared to have no one to blame, no one to complain to, and no excuses to give. We want to be considered adults but yet wish to be accorded the tender courtesies that children desire. If you wish to welcome greatness into your life, you must summon the courage to confront your fears like they don't exist and they will disappear the same way they appeared. You must leverage Absolute Power to challenge yourself without limits and you will discover unimaginable peaks that you never knew existed within you.

To succeed against your fears, you must act against them. To conquer your fears, you must fight against them. To survive despite your fears, you must confront them. To thrive despite your fears, you must double the effort that has brought you thus far. The smallest faith you have is sufficient for you to conquer the biggest challenges on your path to greatness. Call on God with this little faith of yours and you won't believe the magnitude of the miracle that would come forth.

If you think the great people we adore and revere in the world today arrived at greatness without countless leaps of faith against fear, think again. For faith to be absolute, you must be ready to sometimes leap without looking, often jump without guarantees, confidently climb without seeing the top, and religiously make moves without obvious support. Absolute Faith is not acting blindly but rather blindly acting with the unabashed assurance that God cares. The very essence of fear is an affirmation that whatever it is that we are scared of is worth confronting, worth exploring, and worth taking to God in prayer.

Almighty God,

From generation to generation, you promised to never leave nor forsake us, to never let us be put to shame. Through Prophet Isaiah, LORD, you said we will not be burned if we walk through fire, or drown if we are swept away by the ocean. Through King David, you said we should fear not even if walking through the valley of the shadow of death. You promised, LORD, that Your Rod and Staff will comfort us all the days of our lives, and that we shall dwell in Your House forever.

I pray this moment, LORD, for your help to embrace these promises. I pray, LORD, for you to help me accept and dwell on these promises so I may live without fear. To enable me to overcome the challenges, troubles and pain that I have to face, may I be blessed with the wisdom to draw on Your Strength, which you have made available to all.

Almighty Father, I pray for those who are reading this book right now, that you grant them the courage and tenacity required to pass through the fire and not be burned. Grant us the faith to not die even when bitten by snakes and scorpions.

I confess my fears of the unknown, my fears of the uncertainty in my journey en route to fulfillment. May I forge ahead in faith and with love. May I never forget your promises to be with us throughout the ages.

I pray all these through Your Son, Jesus Christ, who conquered fear and death so we may be free from sin, so we may eventually be with you in Spirit every day of our lives. Thank You, Lord, for I strongly believe that you have answered this prayer.

Amen.

Phase 3:

> "If you plan on being anything less than you are capable of being, you will probably be unhappy all the days of your life."
>
> ~Abraham Maslow

Chapter 10

Fifth Element

"Only those who attempt the absurd will achieve the impossible."

~ Albert Einstein

When Abraham Maslow came up with the Hierarchy of Needs in 1943, the whole world embraced it as a more meaningful way of categorizing human desires. Even now, if you are familiar with it, you would applaud this very impressive psychological breakthrough. However, most of us barely ascend beyond the lower elements of this Hierarchy of Needs, which Maslow referred to as the physiological layer. As we work our way through this Hierarchy of Needs, we would discover that people are less fulfilled in the elements that represents the psychological layer.

This indicates that the number of people who actually aim for the fulfillment they claim to desire in life is noticeably slim;

in fact, rather than aiming to thrive, many people only aspire to survive, rather than aiming to at least break even with life, many people make just enough effort to avoid the worst. As a result, the world is now full of people who have fallen short of the general expectations of life, people who are unaware of why they were created in the first place, let alone making the necessary effort to achieve it.

Using a pyramid, Abraham Maslow depicted the levels of human needs as physiological and psychological, stating that when a man begins to ascend the steps of the pyramid, he will soon reach self-actualization. The bottom level of the pyramid are the "Basic Needs" of a human being, which includes air, water, food, sleep, shelter, warmth and excretion. The second level from the bottom is the "Safety Needs", which includes security of body, employment, resources, family, health, property and morality.

The third level from the bottom is the "Love Needs," which includes friendship, family, and sexual intimacy. The fourth level from the bottom is achieved when individuals feel comfortable with what they have accomplished thus far. This is the "Esteem Needs", which includes self-esteem, confidence, achievement, respect of others and respect by others. At the top of the pyramid is the "Need for Self-Actualization," which, according to Maslow, occurs only when an individual has worked his way up the pyramid to reach a state of fulfillment.

Many of us wake up in the morning pursuing means of acquiring the basic human needs and then go to bed planning how to achieve more of it. We work hard for food, water and shelter and then leave our safety to the government we deem unstable, our love to chance which does not exist, and our esteem to be impacted by what others say or do; and then we completely disregard self-actualization, which is the fifth element of Maslow's Hierarchy of Needs. Inasmuch as some people may be quick to respond to issues that require their effort, time and money, our natural tendency as humans is to remain silent and sooth ourselves with the pitiable belief that there are enough able and willing people in the world to make a difference without us. What we believe doesn't really matter until it causes us to conquer the empty vessel of fear and overcome the natural tendency of laziness in unabashed quests to turn our beliefs into action.

Initially coined by Kurt Goldstein, self-actualization means the instinctual need of humans to make the most of their unique abilities and to strive to be the best they can be. In Maslow's words, "Self-actualizing people embraces the facts and realities of the world rather than denying or avoiding them; they are creative and spontaneous in their ideas and actions, and interested in solving problems, especially the problems of others–often a key focus in their lives; they feel closeness to other people, and generally appreciate life; they have a system of morality that is fully internalized and independent of external authority; and finally, they judge others objectively without prejudice". In my journey en route to fulfillment, I have learnt that until we embrace the fifth element, we may not even be able to sustain the other four elements in Abraham Maslow's Hierarchy of Needs. Avoiding the top spot doesn't mean that it doesn't exist. Shying away from it as much as we want will deter fulfillment in life.

What is holding you back from embracing the fifth element? What would you like inscribed on your tombstone when you pass on? How would you like to be remembered? What is the legacy you wish to leave behind for your children and friends? Self-actualization is the opportunity to come out of yourself and get out of your way so that you may begin to welcome greatness into your life. It was scary for me to venture into the grounds that are often associated with heroes and sages, but then, we were all created to be heroes and sages in our own individual way, and being nonchalant, ignorant, or arrogant is contradictory to self-actualization. When we think deeply enough, open enough to leverage Absolute Power, and humble enough to seek the input of competent advisers, it would not take us long to become self-actualizing in ways that are in line with our purpose in life. Self-actualization is not a call to heroism, but rather an expectation of God for having been created at all.

To welcome greatness into your life, you must make every effort to work your way from the first level of Maslow's Hierarchy of Needs to the fifth element. In fact, this is where fulfillment begins, for we were created to continuously strive to be the best we can be, rather than to settle for less; to embrace the fifth element rather than to settle for mere mediocrity. Until we cross over from the physiological layer of Maslow's Hierarchy of Needs to the psychological layer, we will not be ready to venture into the spiritual realms that he omitted in his pyramid. We will not be able to actualize our innermost desires, longstanding dreams, and life purpose. We will not be able to welcome greatness into our lives. Whether you self-actualize or not, the world will remember you for either something or nothing; it depends on how you would like to be remembered when you are long gone–for something or for nothing.

Most of us know exactly what we need to do in order to begin or sustain our individual journey en route to fulfillment. We know what to do in order to conquer the obstacles along the way of self-actualization; however, many of us often remain silent to the innermost urge to take the necessary action. Those with detrimental habits often have consistent urges within themselves to quit these habits, but yet never initiate or continue the process. They agree to the infertility, and even the dangers of these habits, but yet do not make sufficient effort to break these detrimental habits. Despite their innermost urges to take the necessary action, some of them put up strong oppositions when being lovingly urged by others to fulfill the promises they made to themselves.

To sustain your journey en route to fulfillment, self-actualization is a necessity; not an option. Self-actualization is more about others than it is about us. It is more about enabling others to discover their purpose in life, sustain their own journey en route to fulfillment, and welcome greatness into their lives, than it is about us doing so. Self-actualization is meant to complete the self-discovery and self-awareness phases of our journey en route to fulfillment. Abraham Maslow continued: "Self-actualization is the intrinsic growth of what is already in the organism, or more accurately, of what the organism is". In essence, we were created to self-actualize; we just have to break through the empty vessel of fear and apply the rule of engagement to begin. Until then, fulfillment will elude us.

Far into my journey en route to fulfillment, I learnt that fulfillment has four key compartments: Physical, Mental, Emotional and Spiritual. The Physical Compartment is made up of what is seen by the naked eyes; how we look and what we have. It includes our weight and height, our network and net worth. The Mental Compartment is made up of what we know; our intellect, academic qualifications, and level of exposure. This is the compartment that breeds our employable skills; that our assessment by others is based on. The Emotional Compartment is made up of how we feel; our ability to control our feelings. This is the compartment to look for love and hate, revenge and forgiveness, as well as other character flaws and feelings of emotion. Our ability to control our anger, to not be jealous, and to not seek revenge, are all related to how fulfilled we are in the Emotional Compartment.

The Spiritual Compartment is the most demanding of them all, for to be spiritually fulfilled is to no longer live for self but rather for others, and with absolute honour and dignity. A spiritually fulfilled person knows himself so well to avoid temptations of drawback in his journey en route to fulfillment. Whether educated or not, he makes tremendous effort to hone his mental capabilities, often reading books on topics that would position him to share knowledge and inspiration with others. He is fully aware of his emotional challenges and character flaws, and always avoid causing others discomfort and pain. He is so unified with his spirit that he refrains from situations that would cause him to regret or regress in his journey en route to fulfillment.

A spiritually fulfilled person is humbly aware of his own limitations and wholeheartedly acknowledges a Divine Power. He refrains from counting the forgiveness he offers to others and has no second thoughts about the need for him to apologize even before being asked. He seeks to help others overcome challenging situations so they may be able to welcome greatness into their own lives. A spiritually fulfilled person has reached the level of life where nothing else matters but love; and he is known to continually make sacrifices for the betterment of others. While he may end up with wealth, fame and power, he is neither motivated by them nor does he deliberately set out to acquire them. Without a doubt, the Spiritual Compartment of this model is the unacknowledged zenith of Maslow's Hierarchy of Needs.

This Four Compartments of Fulfillment has helped many people to see that even while it may be the highest level of Maslow's Pyramid, self-actualization is only an opportunity to tighten loose ends in these four Compartments of Fulfillment. It is only the beginning of a new phase in our journey en route to fulfillment. While Maslow's philosophy is independent in nature, this philosophy is interdependent in nature, for we cannot be truly fulfilled in life if we lack fulfillment in any of the four compartments. The idea is not to be perfectly fulfilled in every compartment but rather to be content with the effort we are making; it is to be fully aware of the direction we are heading; it is to be self-actualizing enough to sustain our journey en route to fulfillment.

Just as the body gives very clear indications when it is hungry, the mind, heart and soul gives very clear indications when they are weakening. With the exception of the physical state of being which grows naturally, we would barely develop in the other three compartments without very hard work. I have learnt that it is way less tedious to maintain a healthy state of physical being than it is to maintain fulfilling states of being in the mental, emotional and spiritual compartments.

Without much effort, we would still grow physically; but with no effort on our part, we would not grow mentally, emotionally and spiritually. In fact, while we would likely continue to physically grow with minimum effort on our part, we would be dying slowly in the other three states of being if we make no effort at all. Which one of the four Compartments of Fulfillment must you hastily become self-actualizing? To welcome greatness into your life, you must make every effort to not lag behind in the sharpening of your mind, broadening of your heart, and nourishment of your soul.

Irresponsiveness is the highest form of irresponsibility. To not respond when called upon to do the least possible for others is pitiable. But to completely disregard the innermost urge within us to do the least possible for ourselves and others is despicable. This is often the root causes of regret, guilt, unhappiness, and depression. Self-actualization is not about becoming rich or famous, neither is it about becoming a sage or hero. But rather, it is about doing the small things that we are compelled from within to do for the benefit of ourselves and others. It is to love and encourage others in the areas of life that we may be struggling in. It is to mentor a youth rather than join the band of complainers who whine about their lack of respect. It is to do something for somebody even when it may be inconvenient for you. It is to give something to somebody even when you may not have enough for yourself.

In a world where many are numb to their consciences and innermost urges to act, a world where there is an obvious shortage of present day heroes and heroines, many have become complacent even in what they claim to matter. We have urges to take the necessary steps to enhance ourselves, mend a broken relationship, maintain bliss in our marriage, spend quality time with our children and families, and grow in our spirituality, but yet do nothing at all with the hope to somehow not have a broken marriage, a pregnant teenage daughter, or a soon-to-be-dad teenage son. How are you responding to that innermost urge to advance your career, grow your business, or become more disciplined in your finances, eating habits, and time management? How are you responding to your innermost urge to serve at the local food bank, keep in contact with your relatives and use your talents to serve in your community?

Destiny has nothing to do with chance, but rather the outcome of a slew of choices that we have made in life. It is not something that is bestowed upon us, but rather something we create for ourselves. God may have plans to prosper you but not when you are wasting your available time lazing about. A good gauge of your level of self-actualization is reflected in the number of people who look up to you for support, guidance and inspiration. How self-actualizing would your friends and family consider you to be? How determined are you to "fight the good fight, finish the race, and keep the faith", as Apostle Paul puts it? I have learnt that if we honestly listen to our innermost self, we would clearly hear ourselves telling us how to practically enhance our personality, become an effective leader, and make a difference in the lives of others. Being created in the image and likeness of God means that we have an open communication with God, and thus, playing ignorance about what the world expects of us is preposterous.

Without a mirror, and even if we choose to ignore feedback from those around us, we can still clearly identify those growth-deterring habits and character traits that our innermost self is urging us to eliminate in order to welcome greatness into our lives. I know this because the innermost urges to be kind, loving, wise, encouraging, spiritual, gentle, joyful, compassionate, peaceful, humble, faithful, and patient never ceased in me during those years when I was consumed by self only. Even though everything I did everyday was to nurture my ego, I was reminded by the God in me to change my ways, to live for things greater than myself. Everyday that I lived for myself, I was consistently urged to love my neighbour as myself. And every time I failed to do so, I was pricked by my conscience. I will forever be grateful for God's love and grace.

Self-Actualization may be a high calling, but it is an achievable one too. Those who are lagging in their journey en route to fulfillment should first examine the consistency of their actualization. Self-actualization means that you are always making every effort to change your way of being, rather than attempting to change the situation. It means that you are very committed to changing your approach to others rather than trying to change the approach of others to suit your comfort. You can only begin to self-actualize after going through the Self-Discovery and Self-Awareness phases. To self-actualize, you must know who you are and where you are going in life, unlike the average individual who goes through life with no clue about his purpose in life.

If you are a forgetful person, it is self-actualizing to always create a to-do list and post it where it is bound to serve as a reminder. If you are someone who is slow to listen, impatient to speak, and quick to become angry, which is the exact opposite of what Apostle James advised in his biblical book, then it is self-actualizing to be quick to repent and quick to apologize, especially when confronted by those who care enough to do so. Self-actualization means the tireless pursuit of knowledge, the humble acceptance of advice, the sincere expression of apology, and the unconditional offer of forgiveness. Self-actualization means to be prayerful, hopeful and thankful. It means to wake up with your life purpose in mind and go to bed with it still on your mind. It means to make every day count, every life honourable and every thing worth the while.

The easiest things to find in life are excuses for not doing what we should be doing. It is to complain about everything, and to blame someone else for everything. Self-actualizing people are immunized against these. They are quick to apologize rather than make excuses. They would take action rather than complain, and accept accountability rather than blame others. What is holding you back from executing the actions that are necessary for you to achieve your purpose in life? The urge to self-actualize is in everyone because everyone desires fulfillment in life, whether they acknowledge it or not. Many people are stuck in the first few elements of Maslow's Pyramid because their detrimental mindsets were formed based on the impact of unfortunate childhood experiences that hinders fulfillment, preconceived notions that leads no where.

It must have been hard for the people we consider great to keep doing whatever it is that made us consider them great. Perhaps, most of them never considered themselves great because of the fears and challenges they must have been struggling with. But without a doubt, the difference between them and others who choose to maintain the status quo is that they decided to answer the call of life while others chose to ignore it. They decided to make a move while others chose to excuse themselves. They decided to stand up and step in while others decided to stand down and step out. Whether you decide to shout or shrink, fight of flight, it is the same God that created us all. It is now up to us to accomplish our purpose in life or leave it to chance that does not exist. To welcome greatness into our lives, wisdom demands that we pay more attention to our subconscious than to our conscious, for in our subconscious lie our innermost beauty, our purpose in life, and the wealth of wisdom we require to make it happen.

We may fall short in some of our activities, but absolute failure is when we make no effort to rise after the fall. It is to give up without even trying, without making enough effort to press onwards. We assume the position of a failure when we act without being considerate towards others and when we speak without the humility of first examining ourselves. To sustain our journey en route to fulfillment, we must be willing to take some actions strictly by faith and not always by sight. While our actions must always be preceded by very careful thoughts, fulfillment lies, not only in the thinking and strategizing, but in the diligence of our action, and regardless of the outcome.

If you would like to become a high school teacher because of the love and concern that you have for the youth, then you should start making plans to realize this dream rather than being intimidated by the requirements. If you are compelled by your spirit to speak more often in public places because of the inspirational messages you have to share, then you should start seeking opportunities to speak at places that may be less intimidating, like schools and churches. What is your dream that seems to never go away? What is your subconscious urging you to actualize right now? What are the excuses that you are using to hold yourself back from the fifth element?

When I became a Christian in 1998, some of the people who were very close to me told me that I was not going to last long as one. They felt that I was too steeped in sin that even if there was a God who would forgive so much, I had crossed too many lines to be forgiven. As I began disengaging myself from the categories of friends that were hindrances in my journey, one of them said to me, "Let's see how long this spiritual thing would last". Although a few others did not have the courage to voice their opinions so bluntly, they insinuated the same thing as well. They were right, for I could not have done it alone because by ourselves we can do nothing. To have arrived thus far in my journey en route to fulfillment, I had to leverage Absolute Power.

People may be right about you when they say you cannot achieve whatever it is you are pursuing. This is why you must leverage Absolute Power as mentioned in an earlier chapter. It is unwise to set out on a journey alone without faith in God and openness to the support of others. People were right about me being steeped in too many sins, about me having crossed too many lines; but they were wrong about the level of capability that we all have within us to break barriers, to conquer mountains, to cross oceans, to attain greater heights. They were wrong about the astounding ability human beings have to change their mindsets at will and to change the course of their lives forever. They were wrong about the capabilities we have within us to effectuate groundbreaking character changes, about the determination we have to welcome greatness into their lives. Indeed, this is the only thing we have control over; our mindsets. A decade after my baptism, I was chatting with an old friend who I hadn't seen since the days of my rebellion, and he said, "Alex, if you could have changed from those terrible ways of yours, then the devil still has a chance".

The self-discovery phase in my journey en route to fulfillment was an emotional strain on me as it is on most people as well. It was an emotional strain because it required an in-depth exploration of my mindset; it required me to face the most painful parts of my childhood that resulted in my mindset having being initially shaped in a way that is contradictory to my innermost being. The self-awareness phase may not have been as tedious as the self-discovery phase, but it was certainly a mental strain nonetheless. It required me to pay attention to everything that I thought of, everything that I exposed myself to, and everything that I said. I had to be aware of how I communicated with other people, the places I frequented, and the people I hung out with. This is the phase where some people quit the marathon of life for the race of desire, regardless of how far they may have come. I have learnt that the journey en route to fulfillment is a continuum; as soon as you stop being self-aware, your old way of being will eventually creep back on you. This is the importance of self-actualization.

The self-actualization phase, however, is different from the prior two phases because it requires more physical effort than mental and emotional efforts. Imagine the joy of living a life of purpose, of doing exactly what you were created to do, of enabling others to find the joy that lack in their lives. The more I actualize things that are in line with my purpose in life, the more I derive fulfillment. It is this fulfillment that enables us to touch the pinnacle of our existence, to welcome greatness into our lives. This is where spirituality begins, for how could anyone ever claim to be spiritual without self-discovery, self-awareness, and self-actualization.

If there was ever a time for you to embrace your purpose in life, it is now. You may have discovered your purpose in life in the self-discovery phase and got used to it in the self-awareness stage. But now, the self-actualization phase is where you get to make it happen. The Fifth Element is an opportunity to finally live for something and be prepared to die for something. In the words of Og Mandino, "I am here for a purpose and that purpose is to grow into a mountain, not to shrink to a grain of sand. Henceforth will I apply all my efforts to become the highest mountain of all and I will strain my potential until it cries for mercy. Beginning from today, treat everyone you meet as if they were going to be dead by midnight. Extend to them all the care, kindness and understanding you can muster, and do it with no thought of any reward. Your life will never be the same again".

If there was ever a time to step out of your comfort zone and step up in Abraham Maslow's Hierarchy of Needs, it is now. If there was ever a time to welcome greatness in every Compartment of Fulfillment in your life, it is now. As you attain this level in your journey en route to fulfillment, you will find that it is only the beginning of even greater things in your life. You will find out that the fifth element is nothing but the beginning of a whole new level of being. You will discover that it is nothing but an honourable entrance into the spiritual compartment of fulfillment. Self-actualization is something you are going to need for the rest of your journey en route to fulfillment.

Almighty God,

What can I actualize without your grace, mercy and compassion? What can I claim to have done were it not for your love and support that I am sometimes oblivious to? Who am I without you? What is any achievement if not to bring you glory?

Thank you, Father, for imbibing in me everything that I need to achieve whatever you have put on my heart to do. Thank you for creating me with the talents I need to achieve my purpose in life.

Please forgive me in instances where I have allowed the empty vessel of fear to deter me from self-actualizing. Forgive me in instances where I have claimed the glory for self-actualization. Forgive me, Lord, in instances where I have refused to help others be self-actualizing.

May I recognize self-actualization not as the end of my journey en route to fulfillment but rather as the beginning of yet another phase in my journey to live life to the fullest as you expect of me.

Help me, Lord, to look past self-actualization to self-fulfillment. Prepare me for the next phase of my journey, and may I sojourn keeping in mind everything that I have learnt thus far so that I may successfully arrive at the ultimate destination when it is all said and done.

Thank you for listening to my prayer, which I offer to you through Jesus Christ our Lord.

Amen

Chapter 11

Greatness at Work

> **"We are what we repeatedly do.**
> **Excellence, therefore, is not an act, but a habit".**
> **~ Aristotle**

Let's face it, whether appropriate or not, our career has a lot to do with the first impression people have about us. In fact, whether intentionally or unintentionally, people will judge us based on general opinions of what we do for a living or where we work. Our career is a conversation starter, a door opener, and our lifeline. Consider a person who goes to bed at 10:00 P.M., wakes up at 6:00 A.M., leaves home for work at 7 A.M., arrives work at 8 A.M., and then leaves work at about 5 P.M. to arrive back home at 6:00 P.M. Based on this schedule, that person spend about 70% of his or her 16 wake hours pursuing a career, besides the time he or she spends thinking or talking about it during the weekend and while away from work!

This is why we must ensure that our work brings us great satisfaction; otherwise, our attempts to sustain our journey en route to fulfillment in the remaining 30% of our wake hours may be futile. In fact, we are generally going to be as happy in life as we are in our career, for if what we spend about 70% of our time doing is not in line with our purpose in life, it will be a more tedious journey en route to fulfillment. A well paying job does not guarantee satisfaction. And if the job hinders opportunities to welcome greatness into our lives, then it will also hamper our journey en route to fulfillment. This is why it is very important that we align our profession with our purpose in life in order to maximize our efforts and resources. If you are one of those who consistently complain about their careers–places of work, bosses, coworkers, organizational cultures and everything related to it, you will be unable to welcome greatness into your life. This limiting attitude is not only a hindrance to the fulfillment that you seek, but also a recipe for failure in your current and future careers.

God created each of us with the perfect mix of strengths and weaknesses that are suitable for specific careers; specific careers that would allow us to welcome greatness into our lives on a daily basis. While we may sometimes have to go through other jobs to arrive at this suitable career, we have a greater chance of excelling at work when we finally land the suitable job–a job that requires the utilization of our natural strengths and weaknesses. An unsuitable job is bound to make your journey en route to fulfillment more challenging than it would have been if your career was in line with your purpose in life. If you do not see how your career fits into your purpose in life, then it is likely hindering your journey en route to fulfillment.

With his remarkably high level of faith, passion, integrity and diligence, Martin Luther King Jr. would have likely excelled in any career–whether as a bus driver, baker, nurse or baseball player. However, his natural talent of being an eloquent orator enabled him to excel even more in public speaking and preaching. In his career as a preacher, he had more opportunities to display and develop his natural abilities, and to gain more control over his strengths and weaknesses, which enabled him to be fulfilled at what he did for a living. It is this fulfillment that, in turn, enabled him to sustain the greatness he was destined for. How are you using your mix of strengths and weakness to sustain the greatness you are destined for? In the words of Honore de Balzac, "An unfulfilled vocation drains the colour from a man's entire existence." This is the critical point in your journey where you need every capacity within you to sustain it; and if your current job is way more draining than fulfilling, what are you waiting for to do something about it?

Greatness at work is not about being the boss. It is not about being in charge. It is not about making lots of money and exerting lots of influence. But rather, it is about making consistent effort to be better at what you do, to be supportive of your organizational goals, to be encouraging to your employers and employees, and to love everyone in your workplace regardless of the differences between you and them. It is to consider your job as a service to God even if you feel unappreciated, unvalued and underpaid. To be great at work means to be known for humility, servitude, contentment and other principles that many people desire and respect but only a few people make the necessary effort to possess. To sustain your journey en route to fulfillment, you must ensure a strong linkage between your career and your purpose in life, for your career is meant to help you to fulfill your purpose in life, and not to hinder you from fulfilling it.

In the words of Mark Sullivan, "To find a career to which you are adapted by nature, and then to work hard at it, is about as near to a formula for success and happiness as the world provides. One of the fortunate aspects of this formula is that, granted the right career has been found, the hard work takes care of itself. Then hard work is not hard work at all." In essence, if you won't do your current job for free should money not be an issue, then you are yet to land your perfect career. Many of the people who end up arriving at the pinnacle of careers that are not in line with their purpose in life are often dejected throughout the duration of the career and then depressed upon retirement. And unless they come to the awesome realization that it is never too late to begin another career all over again, their dejection and depression will eventually result in illnesses that often shorten lifespan.

Despite some surveys and statistics citing inadequate compensations and insufficient appreciation as the main reasons for the consistently declining rates of job satisfaction in the world today, it is not entirely so. Many people are unsatisfied with their careers because they are in the wrong ones; they are working in the fields that are not aligned with their strengths and weaknesses, jobs that are not enabling them to fulfill their purpose in life. This is often as a result of parents ignorantly grooming their children from infancy for jobs that may never bring fulfillment to their children, or people accepting job offers only because of the associated prestige and income. This goes back to inception, back to the inconvenient truth. It goes back to the lack of vision, the prevailing ignorance of not knowing what our purpose in life is. It goes back to the arrogance of not having accepted more informed advice, and the nonchalance of not having paid enough attention to the warning signs on the highway of life. If you do not know how what you are doing directly impacts the life of another person, you are labouring in vain and your career will hinder your journey en route to fulfillment.

Those who are in the wrong careers often find slight excuses to stay away from work. They complain about their boss, coworkers and everyone and everything at work. It is harder for them to adapt to changes because they feel threatened by everything.

They shout for joy on Fridays and moan aloud on Mondays. Even while at work, they could barely wait to leave before their regular, paid shift is over. Some claim to be 'very busy' with 'work-related' activities that seem to yield no results, and then wonder why they never seem to be recognized or promoted. If we were to ask your fellow employees about the level of dedication and determination they see in you at work, what would they say? What would your spouse say about your attitude towards your boss and workplace, the place that literally helps you to sustain your livelihood?

Those who excel in their careers are those who can't wait to wake up in the morning because of the impact they are motivated to make in the world. They are doing what they enjoy doing or, due to their appreciation for life, have wilfully developed an unabashed passion for it. They are enthusiastic about their work and are committed to doing it with all their hearts regardless of the pay and work environment. If you love your work, you will likely become one of the best workers in that field. I have come this far in my journey en route to fulfillment because my career is my purpose in life. While my previous careers provided me with opportunities to develop my skills and experiences, the personal satisfaction I derived from them is incomparable with the one I am deriving from doing what I was born to do. Every job could be a stepping stone towards greatness if we are open, humble, diligent, and determined enough to learn as much as possible from the work and its associated challenges.

To sustain your journey en route to fulfillment, you must consistently work towards creating a great day at work regardless of whatever happens at home, on your way to work, or at work itself. Make every effort to truly respect your leaders and every other person at work regardless of any attitude that a chaotic day may be displaying through them. Assume every task with passion, quickly appreciating it as an honourable opportunity to serve. Whether you consider your work a perfect career or not, you are still able to become great at it. It is this attitude that will help you to generate the energy and enthusiasm needed to welcome greatness into your life. It is this attitude that will help you to prepare and secure other job opportunities that may be more aligned with your natural strengths and weaknesses.

To welcome greatness into your life, make every effort to protect your integrity. Consistently apply more than due diligence in every situation. Make "going the extra mile" part of your daily routine because of the mere possibility that some people around you may be dealing with more overwhelming workloads and personal challenges than you are. Do not only do what you are paid for, but also what you should probably be paid for, without actually expecting to be paid for it. Greatness at work is a mindset; an attitude. It has nothing to do with your work environment, the leadership experience of your boss or the job itself. While these are certainly nice to have, they are not valid excuses for not making the effort that is necessary to welcome greatness into your life. The work environment may not be as comfortable as we expect it to be and our boss may lack the required experience to intentionally contribute towards our personal and professional development, but the choice to either welcome greatness through our careers or not, is 100% in our hands.

To sustain your journey en route to fulfillment, make it part of your daily routine in your career to keep yourself informed through every medium of communication that exists in the company, as well as through external sources so that you are able to share knowledge with everyone else. Instead of evading opportunities to serve with responses like "I don't know", be committed to knowing and offer to find out for your colleagues and clients. Instead of saying or even thinking, "This matter does not concern me", choose to be loyal to your employer by warm-transferring every matter to where it belong. In and out of work, be responsible, eager, accountable, trustworthy, diligent, determined and passionate. This is greatness at work! This is greatness in life!

Always be on the alert for cues, clues and feedback on how you may be able to do things better. Pursue feedback because it is the breakfast of champions. Immunize yourself against the outbreak of complaining about everything, blaming everyone, and making excuses in every situation. Whatever your job is, make every effort to impress yourself everyday by how well you do it. You should work at it more with your heart than with your hands, more with your head than with your mouth. Wallowing in self-pity because of your job or situation remains the lowest level that you can ever assume in life. Whether you are formally recognized for the effort you make at work or not, you should remember that your career is a huge component of your journey en route to fulfillment, and thus must consistently make the changes that are necessary for you to derive satisfaction from it.

Since your manager is likely busier than you are, consistently take initiatives to support the goal of your company. Keep your manager out of matters that you can handle and, in order to minimize his or her list of surprises, provide him or her with prompt updates on your successes and challenges. The energy you need to excel at work is generated by passion, and passion is generated by an unquenchable desire to execute the things that you strongly believe in. In our journey en route to fulfillment, every job we do along the way counts. We just have to ensure it is leveraged as a stepping stone to sustain our journey. Who would have thought that Jesus Christ who came into the world with the prophesied purpose to seek and save the lost would have carpentry in His resume? But that was one of the jobs he did before becoming a Preacher. He may have also been a gardener too.

Almighty God,

Thank you for the concept of work even though it is sometimes burdensome. Thank you for giving us the opportunity to earn a living and make a difference at the same time. Thank you, Lord, that we are able to use our skills and talents to help make the world a better place through the works of our hands.

Please help me to accept my lot in life and yet not settle for less in my career. Help me to be the best that I can be and yet still aim to be better. May I not be complacent in my position. May I be humble towards everyone around me. May I be open to the feedback of others. May I, Lord, do my job so well that it brings you honour.

For those who are out of work right now, I pray that you bless them with opportunities to serve, opportunities to be engaged in the development of others through the work of their hands. For those who are struggling with their work right now, either because of unfairness, stress, illness and other challenges of life, I pray you grant them peace. Help us all to learn more about you from our work, to see you often at our workplaces and to be good stewards and representatives of Jesus Christ even at work.

Thank you, Lord, for the concept of work, and may excellence be our portion now and evermore.

Amen.

Chapter 12

Power of Integrity

> **"One of the truest tests of integrity is its blunt refusal to be compromised."**
>
> **~ Chinua Achebe**

Have you ever wondered why there is such a remarkably low level of integrity in our societies? Have you ever wondered why there are so many people, organizations, businesses and even governments who give their words so easily and yet have no intention of keeping them? Have you ever been impacted by the irresponsibility of those who do not wish to be held accountable for their actions? What has become of integrity in our societies? It is always wise to direct a question like this to ourselves, for the society is only a reflection of the people in it.

What do you think about the lack of integrity demonstrated by medical doctors who smoke, law enforcement officers who accept bribes, and politicians and public servants who embezzle public funds? What about the judges who withhold information about conflicts of interest during trials, mechanics who steal functional engine parts from the automobiles they were paid to repair, religious leaders who do not practice what they preach, and those who claim to be spiritual but yet clearly contribute to the moral decay of the world? In our journey en route to fulfillment, self-actualization is unsustainable without absolute integrity. Every accomplishment that lacks integrity is only temporal and unsustainable. It will only last as long as your lie does, for the truth will always prevail no matter what. Integrity is one of those honourable qualities that are non-negotiable. You either have it or you don't.

While the lack of integrity demonstrated by some politicians may be very obvious because of the media whose integrity is also a question these days, the lack of integrity in our societies is now an infectious epidemic that is eroding the character of many people and preventing them from welcoming greatness into their lives. This includes parents, teachers, religious leaders, government officials, celebrities, business executives, traders and salespeople. Due to the common quest for money, fame and power, the integrity of many have gone sour and the laws that once held our societies together are gradually disintegrating. This was how I lived my life for more than half of it until I began my journey en route to fulfillment.

Besides being one of the values written down in national anthems, emblems, official codes of conduct and courthouses, acts of integrity are now rare in schools which are meant to be places for learning, courthouses which are meant to be places for justice, government officials who are meant to be advocates for the people, and religious leaders who are meant to model integrity for their congregations. These days, you do not have to search to find someone who is bent on selling you something under a false pretence or someone who is fraudulently cutting corners in his or her taxes. You do not have to search to find someone who is trying to get a job with a falsified resume or someone who is telling a lie to look good. You do not have to search to find someone who is attempting to assume the credit of another or someone who is wickedly pointing you towards the wrong direction. Even most relationships are based on false pretences, and then we wonder about the astronomical rate of divorce in our societies!

It is now common to find major corporations who declare exorbitant profits in a year, and then in the following year, fire their executives for cooking the books. It is now common to find employees who regularly steal time and resources from their employers as well as employers who regularly overwork their subordinates with the duties of other employees who were retrenched. It is now common to find pastors and evangelists who expect significantly more sacrifices from their congregations than they are willing to make themselves. Some of these religious leaders even expect more financial sacrifices from their congregations than what God expects. One thing about integrity is that it always has a way of catching up with those who lack it. Just ask those who are imprisoned for their nefarious acts and they would tell you that it is only a matter of time before what you think would never catch up with you eventually does.

In my days of rebellion, I thought I was the smartest and brightest. At least, it was what the shallow people I associated myself with always made me to believe. Most of what I did was "successful" and most of what I said "came true". Lying was my language and deception was my lifestyle. What did it matter if I told a lie to gain some material wealth as long as I gave some to the poor? Robin Hood did the same thing. What did it matter if I told some lies to satisfy my promiscuous desires? I wasn't planning to marry any of them anyway. What does it matter if I cheated in my exams? Is it not getting the certificate that truly matters? Looking back now, I wonder if I ever told any truth during those dark years. This is still how many people live their lives–doing things based on shallow excuses like "Robin Hood did it". To sustain your journey en route to fulfillment, it is high time that you scanned your life at this very moment and ensure that you have tightened every loose end with regards to integrity.

To welcome greatness into our lives, we must immunize ourselves against so many things that seem to have become the norm in today's societies. We must make every effort to restrain ourselves from situations that causes adrenalin to rush and abstain from opportunities others may consider golden. According to John F. MacArthur and John F. MacArthur Jr., in their book, The Power of Integrity: Building a Life Without Compromise, "We live in a world of compromise–in a society that has abandoned moral standards and Christian principles in favour of expediency or pragmatism. The underlying philosophy is based on accomplishing goals by whatever means are necessary. This self-centred perspective should have as its motto: 'If it works for you, then do it'–a notion that inevitably leads to compromise; guilt and remorse are nonfactors in determining behaviour." While we may now live in an era that has unfortunately accepted the lack of integrity is some cases, must we also?

Integrity is the most valuable asset we can ever possess and the most needed companion in our journey en route to fulfillment. Without it, greatness will elude us. It is the highest form of honesty, truthfulness and openness. It is the steadfast adherence to strict moral and ethical principles. It is the unquestionable soundness of moral character. Words like "white lie", "partial truth" and "blue collar crimes" were formed by those who were bent on diluting the Power of Integrity to excuse their lack of it. If you wish to welcome greatness into your life, you must first welcome integrity into it. In fact, integrity and greatness go hand in hand. This was one of the most difficult concepts to grasp when I began my journey en route to fulfillment. I was awestruck to know that it was way more than just telling the truth; it is an indisputable demarcation between those running the race of desire and those running the marathon of life.

People will question your integrity when you make a promise and do not keep it and when you say one thing and do something else. People will question your integrity when you are present in places where you should be absent from and absent from places where you should be present. People will question your integrity when you think and see things that you should not and when you do not make enough effort to fulfill your responsibilities as a citizen, spouse, parent, worker, leader, supervisor, manager, pastor, evangelist, or business owner. When we go to bed absolutely satisfied that we have fostered integrity in every area of our lives throughout the day, we will always sleep well regardless of our challenges, and we will wake up the next day even more determined to dwell in the Grace of God.

While we tend to create a false sense of integrity by comparing ourselves to people with watered down versions of integrity, an accurate measure of our integrity is easily derived by comparing who we portray ourselves to be to who we truly are, by comparing the effort we make in everything we do to the effort we are really capable of making, and by comparing our contribution to humanity with the contribution we are really capable of making. How often do you knowingly compromise your integrity? How often do you go back to correct instances where you unknowingly lacked integrity upon realizing your mistake? How blunt are you when tempted with "golden opportunities" that compromises what you claim to stand for?

Like many others, upholding integrity was and remains one of the most daunting challenges in my journey en route to fulfillment. Like many others, I grew up in an environment that remarkably lacked it, with examples of integrity scarce everywhere I turned to. Saying something and doing something else was my way of being as long as it did not impact me. I often excused my lack of integrity with the thought that no life was in danger by my nonchalance, arrogance and ignorance. I believed it wasn't a big deal to lie if no life was at stake. I believed that integrity only comes to play when under someone's authority. I believed that I could have some integrity with my mom and none with my manager at work. I lied so much that I eventually had no clue about who I was. The idea of double life, in itself, lacks integrity.

Integrity is not something you can possess partially; you either have it or you don't. When you lack integrity in the job you are paid to do, you lack integrity, period! You cannot claim to lack integrity at work and not in your personal life. This is because integrity has nothing to do with the environment or circumstance, but rather everything to do with your character. Before pointing a finger at someone else for lacking integrity, it is wise to question your own authenticity. Before accusing the local pastor of mismanaging the funds of his church, you should question your integrity regarding the contributions you make and the finances of your own household. How well are you managing the funds God has blessed you with? When Jesus Christ said, "Let he who has not sinned throw the first stone", he was calling us to be mindful of our unjustified quickness to accuse others, especially when we lack integrity as well.

Before you accuse anyone of anything, you should question the integrity of your own behaviour to avoid being a hypocrite. When you think no one is watching you, which websites do you surf? Do you consistently harbour lustful and covetous thoughts in your mind? Do you always devise wicked plans and schemes against those you claim to love? How often do you think of and look at other people in disrespectful and inappropriate manners? Integrity is not only about what you do or do not do, but also about what you feel, see, think, touch and listen to. You welcome greatness into your life when you continuously develop your abilities to control your desires and your senses; when you make every effort to be self-aware and self-controlled.

What would your young children think of your integrity when they become adults? Since it is in death that our secrets are uncovered and our lives are laid bare, how would people rate your integrity when you pass on? Regardless of how you may have presented yourself in your lifetime, your true character will be exposed when you pass on, and your loved ones will either have to rejoice in your accomplishments or bear the painful embarrassment of whatever dirt you accumulated while alive. To die with the mindset that no one will ever know what we did or who we truly were is a regrettable state to be when returning back to God. How ignorant is it for us to ever think that our Creator is unaware of the contents of our hearts?

If we must show off anything about ourselves, then let it be our integrity, for it is our most valuable asset. Let it be our quickness to respond to others, to fulfill our responsibilities, to show up for life, and the diligence with which we execute our obligations. Let it be to stand up for what is right even when everyone else think otherwise. Let it be to die for what we believe in even if we die alone. Let it be to be absolutely truthful to ourselves even when everyone else is in doubt. This is the level of integrity that is required for your journey en route to fulfillment. There is no alternative. Until we are making every effort to consistently protect our integrity, it will not stand the test of time; it will be demolished by our laxity. Integrity is one of those qualities we lose without even knowing it.

How are you modelling integrity for your family, boss, employees, peers, congregation, community, and everyone else around you? How closely aligned are your life and your doctrine? How would your spouse, boss and co-workers rate your integrity on a scale of 1 to 5, with 5 being the highest? Ask them and they would be honoured to share with you. This is a test where anything below 5 is unacceptable. Like Francis Bacon Sr. once said, "It's not what we eat but what we digest that makes us strong; not what we gain but what we save that makes us rich; not what we read but what we remember that makes us learned; and not what we profess but what we practice that gives us integrity." Basically, we build integrity for ourselves by fostering those principles that everyone admires but only a few have the courage to foster.

To welcome greatness into our lives, we must consistently leverage Absolute Power to ensure absolute integrity. We must consistently strive to be a man or woman whose integrity is beyond reproach. We must make every effort to ensure our lives and doctrines match, and that we persevere in them. We must live our lives in ways that when people think of us, they think of integrity. Without knowledge, we may perish. Without integrity, we don't even exist at all. It is not necessarily what we do that affirms our integrity, but rather our mindset; what we often think about. Integrity is telling ourselves the truth wholeheartedly and living it unswervingly.

In my journey en route to fulfillment, I have learnt that we never fall short of any goal, but rather the passion to keep the goal alive, the effort to maintain a forward momentum, the integrity to effectively lead ourselves and others, the diligence to tighten loose ends and the openness to accommodate (not necessarily accept) other people's opinions. To welcome greatness into our lives, we must consider integrity to be our most valuable asset. In the words of Jesus Christ, "Enter through the narrow gate; for wide is the gate and broad is the road that leads to destruction, and many enter through it. But small is the gate and narrow the road that leads to life and only a few find it". If the road that you are travelling on is broad, then you may be heading the wrong direction.

Most of the qualities that make people great are offspring of integrity: trust, honesty, accountability, hard work, determination, leadership and compassion. These and similar qualities that are required for us to sustain our individual journey en route to fulfillment can only become part of us when we strive to be people of integrity. Until we are truthful with ourselves, we cannot be truthful to others. Until we foster integrity on a consistent basis, we cannot embody other character traits that are required to welcome greatness into our lives. Until we make integrity our closest companion, our journey en route to fulfillment will be futile.

What will be said of us when we depart this world would be reflective of our selflessness or selfishness, our courage or cowardice, our determination or laziness, our honesty or dishonesty, our integrity or the lack of it. The people who are not guided by principles and integrity would do anything, watch anything, listen to anything, say anything, read anything, play with anything, go anywhere, and then end up dying for nothing. It is what we leave behind in terms of integrity, compassion and demeanour that count way more than any tangible possession we will out to those we leave behind when we pass away.

All that is required for you to shine enough for others to see, for you to be the salt of the earth and the light of the world as God expects, is to be guided by the conviction that you were made in the image and likeness of God. It is this conviction that will motivate you to ensure your conscience is consistently at peace with your soul. It is this conviction that will make you disregard whatever repercussions may result from being truthful. This is the Power of Integrity; the master key to every door on your journey en route to fulfillment.

Almighty God,

I am in awe of your integrity,
for every word you spoke since time began
continues to manifest in our lives.
I am in awe of your integrity, for the promises
you made even before we were born
remains ours to grab.

I confess my lack of integrity in areas of my
life that I may even be unaware of -
be it in my personality, leadership,
marriage, parenting, spirituality;
be it in my relationships, health & wellness, academics, career;
be it in my taxes, finances and businesses.
I confess excusing my lack of integrity with
uncompassionate and uncaring thoughts;
with deeds of selfishly motivated philanthropy.

Thank you for your mercy, for still being so generous
to me with your love and your grace;
for showering your blessings on me even
in areas where I lack integrity.
Thank you for forgiving my self-righteous thoughts
of comparing myself to other people who I arrogantly
believed lacked integrity more than I do.

Father, Lord, please continue to help me in
this journey en route to fulfillment.
Please forgive my lack of integrity in (list 3 very
specific areas that you require help with)
May I seize every opportunity to model
integrity for myself and others.
May I begin to wholeheartedly stand by my
words regardless of the consequences.
May I remain on this journey en route
to fulfillment forever and ever.

Amen.

Chapter 13

Return to Love

> **"The hunger for love is much more difficult to remove than the hunger for bread".**
>
> **~Mother Teresa**

The lowest level we can ever assume in life is to respond to hate with hate, aggression with aggression, and selfishness with selfishness. It is to do unto others what we would rather is not done to us. It is to know and not say, see and not tell, have and not share, feel and not control. It is to live our lives in such a way that only we seem to matter, to go about our daily lives without showing any kind of love to our neighbours, and without thinking, even for just a moment, of our purpose in life and the need for personal growth.

The lowest level we can ever assume in life is to quit on the responsibilities that were designed to give us the fulfillment that people ignorantly pursue in the empty areas of life–like to wickedly quit a marriage in the pursuit of self-gratification regardless of the destructive impact on the family. It is to parent children in ways other than those intended by the Lord, to not recognize or make enough attempt to break the unfortunate vicious cycle that has been tearing down families for generations. It is to hold grudges against others without making concrete plans for resolution, to quarrel and yet have no intention to make peace, to perceive the downfall of others and yet choose to be silent.

The lowest level we can ever assume in life is to make claim to life and yet find nothing to apologize for, nothing to be grateful for, and nothing to be polite about. It is to stand by social laws that support ignorance, excuse laziness, propel selfishness, applaud hastiness, encourage revenge, and enable the systematic elimination of lives through execution, euthanasia and abortion. If we wish to welcome greatness into our lives, we must begin to see life as a journey where our life purpose is to enable the life purpose of other people. We must begin to see life as a process that can only be refined by challenges, as an opportunity for impact that must be passionately seized. We must begin to harness the power of love, for we were created by Love, in love, for love and with love.

Love is one of the most complicated concepts in life. It is one of the most commonly used words and yet the most pronounced lack in the world. It is often misused, misunderstood and misapplied. If the high number of people who claim to understand what love means is near the truth, the world would not be filled with so much hatred. We claim to love our neighbours and yet the world is ravished by wars and rumours of war. Some of us have not even met the neighbours that we claim to love! If we really understand what love means, why is selfishness and greed so rampant? Why are so many marriages ending up in divorce? Why are the rates of murder, robbery, abandonment and every kind of wickedness on the increase?

It seems that as the number of churches, mosques, synagogues and temples which were supposedly founded on love increases, so does the number of hate crimes, single parenthoods, schemes of betrayal, and suicides and homicides; so does pride, greed, disunity and discord. If the world actually understands the concept of love like we claim to, why is the world so full of dejection, deception, depression and destruction? Why is the world so full of atrocities and calamities? As my daughter, Naomi Ihama, said the other day, "Dad, love is just a word. It is what we do that counts". If we must commit ourselves to anything, subject ourselves to anything, or be willing to die for anything, let it be for love, to love and with love; for what other reason do we have to live other than to be deeply involved in the betterment of others.

True love is less of a feeling and more of a healing. It is less of an intention and more of an action. It is less about us and more about the person we claim to love. Our claim to love anyone is meaningless if the love we claim to have is not obvious enough for the person to be assured of our love. You can say you love and care for the younger generation all you want, but if the love you claim to have does not move you to champion a cause for them or volunteer to help in any way, shape or form, it is likely a thought that you harbour to satisfy your conscience which must be pricking you to take action. Love requires you to inconvenience yourself until the fulfillment it brings eventually makes you to be joyful despite the inconvenience.

Whether we give or accept love is a choice we make every moment. If we choose to not give or accept love, we basically choose to be unhappy for that moment; and a succession of these moments will eventually create a life of unhappiness. We may pursue other avenues to attempt filling our love tank, to subdue the lack of love in us, but will ultimately do so in vain. Some of us have the experiences of having received what we thought would make us fulfilled only to be disappointed that if anything, they made the lack of love in our lives more pronounced than before.

The search for love outside ourselves is the most fruitless effort we can ever make. We must search within. We must prepare ourselves to give and receive this ultimate gift of love every moment of our lives. Restraining or refuting it will only cause injury to self and others. Regardless of how precious some things may seem, nothing tangible or intangible can ever fill the vacuum that is meant to be filled by love.

While many people are obviously yet to understand the meaning of love, it is only a few of those who claim to understand it that actually makes choices based on it. Since we were created in the image and likeness of God, then we were all created by Love, in love and with love. But during our upbringing, especially if raised by unloving parents or under unfortunate circumstances that were filled with neglect and abuse, we learnt to hate along the way. Consciously or subconsciously, we began to substitute love for hate, which was why Jesus Christ once remarked, "Because of the increase of wickedness, the love of most will grow cold". The increasing instances of hate in the world have no bearing on the fact that we were created by Love, in love, for love and with love. It is only an indication of how cold people have become because of the wickedness of others. It attests to the fact that only a few people have identified their purpose in life let alone on the journey en route to fulfillment.

At a very young age, when our morals were not yet corrupted, we felt guilty when caught behaving wrongly. But as we grew older, especially when we had been victims of unfortunate circumstances, we were no longer pricked by guilt. It is at this innocent stage of our lives that we consciously or subconsciously choose to love or hate. We attempt to justify our unloving stances by thinking: "Why should I not react in anger when everyone else seems to be angry for less significant matters?" "Why should I share what I have when no one seems to share with me when in need?" "Why should I not take revenge when those around me never forgive my mistakes?" Because of what others do or don't do, many of us have now forgone our natural inclination to love and sadly allowed our hearts and minds to be infiltrated by the hate around us.

To welcome greatness into our lives, we must be willing to return to love. We must be willing to become lovers of all and haters of none. While we may not love enough to allow ourselves to be crucified on a cross like Jesus did, we must be willing to feed the hungry, clothe the naked, parent the orphans, care for the widows, comfort the sick and visit the imprisoned. We must be willing to encourage and impact everyone around us in ways that make them feel loved. We must be willing to love our neighbours, at least, as much as we love ourselves. This is the beginning of greatness, the sustenance of our journey en route to fulfillment.

I have learnt that the highest level of living is to be so connected to God that whatever people do or don't do does not hinder the unconditional love we must give to them, the utmost respect we must accord them, and the voluntary service we must render them. It is to care for others as God does for us, and leave their shortcomings for God to deal with. According to Charles Morgan, "There is no surprise more magical than the surprise of being loved. It is God's finger on man's shoulder." To validate your purpose in life, you must ensure that it is based on love for other people; you must ensure that the outcome of whatever you do stands to benefit mankind as much as it stands to benefit yourself.

True love is born by the consistency of the good we think and do for people in ways that consistently make them feel loved, in ways that, even while challenging to them, turns out to be for their own betterment, our own peace of mind, and the growth of the relationship. The love that is buried in the deepest part of our hearts, with thoughts and actions that are not remarkable enough to demonstrate what we think we feel, is of use to no one. In fact, a verbal attestation of love for anyone, with no action to back it up, is selfishness. It is love of self rather than love of another. Our decision to remain alive must be tied to our decision to love, for if anything is worth living for, it is love. The craziness of the world and the emptiness of lives are all related to the growing lack of love, the undeniable need for love.

True love requires us to alternate between toughness on ourselves and toughness on the people we claim to love. While we may sometimes maintain an imbalance of this fact to our own detriment, it is no longer love when we are consistently tough on ourselves and barely tough on the people that we claim to love. It is no longer love when we are overly tough on others in ways that we do not challenge ourselves. Fear is the absence of love, either for self or for others. Tough love, we have often heard people say, is real love, for love must have a tough element to it or else it is the love of self and not the love of another. When we continuously yield to the detrimental habits of someone who we claim to love for the sake of peace and harmony which may not really exist in the relationship, we are no longer being loving towards that person, but rather loving and protective of ourselves–to the detriment of the relationship. In fact, this is counterintuitive to the love of God, the love God expects us to have for one another. I have learnt that the most beautiful experience in life is that of love. It is to love with everything you have, everything you are, with no restraints, with no expectations. It is to feel loved even when it is unspoken, to know love even when it is disguised. Love makes nothing else seem to matter, not even what may really matter.

"Love is patient, love is kind", Apostle Paul once said. "It does not envy, it does not boast, it is not proud. It is not rude, it is not self-seeking, it is not easily angered, and it keeps no record of wrongs. Love does not delight in evil but rejoices with the truth. It always protects, always trusts, always hopes, and always perseveres. Love never fails." Based on this very profound definition of love, how satisfactory is the love you claim to have for those around you? How loving are you towards yourself? Our obvious feelings of appreciation for others do not automatically translate into love until they are backed by consistent efforts and actions; until what we say or do are selflessly meant to enable the development of the people we claim to love.

Before we claim to love anyone, we must be able and willing to consistently conquer our own natural tendencies of fear, greed, selfishness and laziness so that we may be able to consistently support whomever we claim to love with our openness, courage, selflessness and action. To truly love someone else, we must not only be able and willing to put that person first, but also be open to not being loved in return by that same person. In the words of Leo Buscaglia, "Perfect love is rare indeed–for to be a lover will require that you continually have the subtlety of the very wise, the flexibility of the child, the sensitivity of the artist, the understanding of the philosopher, the acceptance of the saint, the tolerance of the scholar and the fortitude of the certain". I have learnt that to love anyone wholeheartedly, we must love ourselves judiciously.

Despite the ugliness and wickedness of the world, if you love others despite their hate towards you, thank people even for favours and courtesies that may be considered insignificant, and apologize even when you are not in the wrong, your life will begin to blossom like a bunch of roses. Contrary to the natural understanding of man, if you put people ahead of you, they will begin to follow you. If you consider others better than yourself, they will consider you better than everyone else. To welcome greatness into your life, you must act, not according to human understanding, but according to supernatural direction, not according to the norm, but according to the original intention of God for man.

Love and greatness are inseparable. They are one and the same. For while we may be great at what we do, we can only welcome greatness into our lives when our action is motivated by love for others, by love for the world. Look at Mother Theresa, who we may very well call Mother Love: she signed up to be a nun, but resigned herself to demonstrating love for the most unfortunate people in the poorest parts of the world. Look at Martin Luther King Jr., who, compelled by love for the oppressed, literally sacrificed his life for the cause of his people, for the cause of love.

The only way to leave a legacy behind is to be motivated by love, to be guided by love and to die for love. If you are not living a life of love, a life that is void of hate, jealousy, envy, revenge, selfishness and laziness, you will be unable to welcome greatness into your live. In fact, you would have only succeeded in living a life that contradicts your purpose in life. For whatever we achieve in life to be sustainable, it must be founded on love; it must be achieved in harmony with the Holy Spirit, in line with God's plan for us. Whoever steps on others to arrive at the top will sooner or later be brought down by other likeminded people who are aiming for the top as well.

Apostle Paul continued: "Love must be sincere. Hate what is evil; cling to what is good. Be devoted to one another in brotherly love. Honour one another above yourselves. Never be lacking in zeal, but keep your spiritual fervour, serving the Lord. Be joyful in hope, patient in affliction, and faithful in prayer. Share with God's people who are in need. Practice hospitality. Bless those who persecute you; bless and do not curse. Rejoice with those who rejoice; mourn with those who mourn. Live in harmony with one another. Do not be proud, but be willing to associate with people of low position. Do not be conceited. Do not repay anyone evil for evil. Be careful to do what is right in the eyes of everybody. If it is possible, as far as it depends on you, live at peace with everyone."

Love is the only true universal language which is spoken in numerous dialects. It can be heard by the deaf, communicated by the dumb, felt and exuded by the sick, received and delivered by the lame, and is awakening and refreshing to everyone who speaks it. People who continuously learn, practice and speak this language are able to communicate without limitation. If we allow hurt, laziness and pride to deter us from becoming representatives of love, agents of progress and examples of leadership, the destructive direction of the world will remain unchanged. The world and our homes are only reflections of who we are–the level of love we have for ourselves and for others. To welcome greatness into our lives, we must never wait to be loved before expressing the love in our hearts. It is there, despite the rampancy of wickedness.

To welcome greatness into our lives, we must return to love. We must take captive every thought of hate, selfishness, greed, anger, harshness, fear and wickedness. We must be willing to step out of our comfort zones and trust that love never fails. We must be willing to overcome daily temptations of procrastination and intimidation to make that phone call of encouragement, offer comfort to another, and expand our way of thinking for the betterment of others. We must forgive the wrongs against us and strive to be righteous at all times.

The highest calling in life is neither to rule a kingdom nor preside over a nation, but rather to perform daily acts of love even if in the smallest form possible. It is to make daily attempts to put just a smile on the face of another even if there is nothing for you to smile about. Love like never before and your life will shine like never before. Irrespective of how a confrontation may make us feel, we must never aim to take away the dignity of others even when they seem to care less about their own dignity. Greatness demands that we make as much effort to protect the dignity of other people as we make to protect our own. Greatness is love and love is greatness. Both are inseparable, and the journey en route to fulfillment is actually a return to love. The journey is the transformation, but the destination is love.

Almighty God,
You are indeed, love, at its utmost.
You created us with love, for love and by love.
No on can love like you do and no one can be loved like you are.
How insufficient is the love we claim to
have, the love we claim to give.
How conditional, how untrue, how unreal is the love
we claim to have for ourselves and for others.
Thank you for your mercy,
for still being so generous to me with your love and your grace;
for showering your love on me despite my lack of it.
Thank you for forgiving my self-righteous
thoughts of comparing myself to
other people who I arrogantly believed are not as loving as I am.
May I begin to demonstrate love as you expect of me.
May I begin to overcome the obstacles in my return to love.
Lord, may your love for me inspire me all the days of my life,
And help me to become epitome of love for all.
Amen.

Chapter 14

Life to the Fullest

> **"Until an individual can rise above the narrow confines of his individualistic concerns to the broader concerns of all humanity, he is not fit to live."**
>
> **~ Martin Luther King Jr.,**

One of the biggest problems of our generation is not the lack of resources as the media may portray it to be, but rather the despairing gap between the wealthy and the poor, the affluent and the needy, the educated and the ignorant, the wise and the unwise, the loving and the hateful, the generous and the selfish, the compassionate and the vengeful. It must be heartbreaking for God to see the increasing number of people and countries who continue to selfishly and aggressively amass an unimaginable amount of wealth and power with no intention of sharing with the downtrodden. From time immemorial, man has always grieved

God; but God must be grieved even more by the ignorance, nonchalance, and arrogance of this generation, which He has remarkably blessed with amazing technological advancement and abounding resources.

How can one person dare claim to be worth over fifty billion dollars in the same world where millions of people still die of hunger and many more live in inhumane conditions with no shelter, no water, no food, no clothing? How can one country dare to boast of over ten thousand nuclear warheads in the same world where some farmers are unable to afford fertilizers for their crops? Recent statistics indicates that the combined financial wealth of 20 people in the world is over $1,000,000,000! While this is amazing, it is heartbreaking too because hunger still remains the number one issue in the world. It is even more troubling to know that there are 23,000 known nuclear warheads in the world, with two countries owning up to 90% of this stockpile of evil!

We should be ashamed of ourselves for having allowed the world to unfortunately digress this far during our generation, for having allowed ourselves to move from love to hatred, peace to war, awareness to ignorance, and knowledge to foolishness. And if any of us dare to claim ignorance about the aches and pains that the lack of spirituality is causing people in the world today, it would be an indication of either our arrogance or nonchalance. According to Mother Teresa, "We think sometimes that poverty is only being hungry, naked and homeless. The poverty of being unwanted, unloved and uncared for is the greatest poverty. We must start in our own homes to remedy this kind of poverty".

As mentioned in a prior chapter, self-actualization is by no means the height of human existence, but rather only the beginning in the last leg of our journey en route to fulfillment. It is by no means the end of our journey en route to fulfillment, but rather a prerequisite to the final phase. In itself, self-actualization does not bring the fulfillment we desire in life, but rather instrumental in our desire to welcome greatness into our lives. A farmer who has mastered the art of gardening may be blessed with voluptuous harvest year after year, and thus perceived as a self-actualizing person. However, sooner or later, that farmer would begin to have innermost urges to continue the journey en route to fulfillment, not by expanding his empire as the natural tendency would dictate, but rather by giving it away as the supernatural tendency would suggest.

If we are not doing the little we can do with the little we have, we should convicted ourselves for not having done enough to make the world a better place than when we first came into it. While the efforts made by the farmer to achieve so much may be deemed self-actualization, the urge to move from profit to philanthropy is the call to live life to the fullest. We see this happening every now and then with a few moguls of our days stepping down from the affairs of powerful conglomerates to dedicate their lives to humanitarian causes like finding cure for terminal illnesses or fighting against poverty. Some have even given up half of their wealth to support charitable cause, while their families and friends gape in amazement.

To live life to the fullest is not about having it all, but rather about giving it all up for the benefit of others. All we have to offer may be words of encouragement and exhortation, but we would be living life to the fullest if it is all we have to offer. It may be our time, money or effort, but we would be living life to the fullest if it is truly sacrificial on our part. It is the heart with which we offer ourselves and what we have that differentiate between self-actualization and self-fulfillment. It is the heart with which we self-actualize that indicates whether we are only alive or actually living. In the words of Jesus Christ, "Small is the gate and narrow the road that leads to life and only a few will find it". You may have come this far in your journey en route to fulfillment, but are you on what Jesus referred to as the narrow road? Until some of your associates begin to think you are out of your mind because of your sacrifices for humanity, you may not have found the narrow road and small gate.

To live life to the fullest has nothing to do with being rulers of kingdoms, presidents of nations or topmost executives in organizations. It has nothing to do with your job title, what you do, and what others consider you to be. It has nothing to do with the impressiveness of your educational qualifications, material possessions and abounding accolades. But rather, to live life to the fullest is directly tied to your spiritual state of being. It is directly tied to your ability to humbly accept constructive feedback; your ability to not feel threatened or insecure when your space is invaded, when your ignorance is exposed, when your decision is challenged, when your apology is requested, and when your thoughts are provoked. A life that is lived to the fullest is built on a foundation of utmost love, absolute integrity and overwhelming humility. It embodies spirituality at the highest level.

Our challenge is less about finding this small gate and more about being determined enough to go through it when we find it. It is less about the road being narrow and more about the struggle with our egos to remain on it. What we hold dear in our hearts will eventually make or break us. Naked I came into the world, and naked I will be returning back to my Creator. Of what use is hoarding billions of dollars that could be channelled towards eradicating hunger for many generations to come? Of what use is it to have talents if not to expend them for the benefits of others? What people fail to realize is that we don't die fulfilled because we had it all, but rather because we gave it all. This is how Jesus Christ conquered death, how he fulfilled His purpose on earth; by giving up His life on the cross for the benefit of mankind. What are you giving up today so the life of another person may be better tomorrow?

Pity is the person who passes away without having expended himself for the benefit of a worthy cause. It is no wonder that the wealth of those who pass on without having blessed others with it is squandered foolishly by their offspring. The question is not about saving for the future, but rather about being sacrificial in the present. It is about taking up our cross daily and following the Lord, whatever our cross turns out to be. It is about remaining on the narrow road despite our detrimental character traits and external circumstances. It is about being determined enough to continue the journey even if it means fasting for forty days like Jesus Christ did. You can save as much as you want for the future, but not when others are dying of hunger today. Ask Nelson Mandela who sat in jail for twenty-seven years in protest of apartheid and he will tell you what it means to live life to the fullest.

If we were to take a deeper look into our homes and hearts, we would most likely realize that even after coming this far in our journey en route to fulfillment, many of us are still struggling with our egos in areas that should not be so. Many of us are making so much effort to actualize our desires, but then stop short of living life to the fullest so as not to lose the comfort associated with self-actualization. Many of us have allowed exorbitance and wastage to settle in our homes, and greed, envy and jealousy to settle in our hearts, and then assure ourselves of holiness because we volunteer every now and then in a homeless shelter or make regular contributions to the United Way. I know this because I was once a victim of myself for so many years, and I still come across people who have the same self-destructive mindset. How arrogant it is to think that we are absolved of our atrocities because we give part of our loot to the poor.

The reason some of the people portrayed by the media as self-actualizing eventually commit suicide is because they still lacked fulfillment despite having acquired so much wealth, fame and power. This is the bottomless pit that I found myself in over a decade ago. Arriving at the peak of the shallow standards of today's society presented me with two choices: commit suicide or begin the journey en route to fulfillment. I had way more possessions than I needed and had a very strong influence over people to the extent that some caused damage to their souls because of my bad influence over them. Despite all these, the satisfaction derived from wealth, fame and power did not bring me the fulfillment I longed for, for what most people call fame is in fact, notoriety. I know this because the fame I had during the days of my rebellion was narrow, nefarious and notorious. It made me emptier everyday until the point of near death.

It may sound simple, but living life to the fullest is way much more than just inviting your neighbours over for BBQ. It is way much more than making charitable donations to ensure a favourable tax return. It is way much more than sending feeding allowances to your aged parents. It is way much more than having a seat on the board of your local church, community or corporation to enhance your prestige. While these may be honourable acts depending on your motives, you will only be living life to the fullest when you have zero expectation of gratitude or reward; when you have gone so far in your journey en route to fulfillment that you are barely tempted to glorify yourself rather than God who blessed you with the opportunities. You would be living life to the fullest if, despite your remarkable effort, you express appreciation where you should be appreciated, are thankful for opportunities that you may have created for others, and are serving without grumbling.

Until we are willing to spend our only week of vacation to volunteer in one of the leprosy camps in the most remote part of the world, we are yet to understand what it means to live life to the fullest. These are the types of sacrificial acts that makes people smile when death comes knocking; for them to know that they have daringly helped to rescue souls from the horrific grip of the devil, like I was rescued by a few good men. In the words of Horace Mann, "Those who never sacrificed a present to a future good, or a personal to a general one, can speak of happiness only as the blind do of colours". We can never live life to the fullest until we are passionate about helping others to live their lives to the fullest. In fact, our lives will be empty until we consistently seize opportunities to fill up the lives of others.

To live life to the fullest, we must take our eyes off the reward and our minds off the appreciation. We must be consistent in our efforts to be loving, lovely and lovable. We must expect and accept no reward for our sacrifices. We must be willing to watch over everyone including those who may care less about themselves, bless everyone including those who may be cursing others, and support everyone including those who may heed no advice. It is then, and only then, would we begin to live life to the fullest. Everyone wants to be an angel, but many of us often forget that angels are neither paid nor rewarded. Angels work, neither for reward nor recognition, but in appreciation of God's love.

Coined by Jesus Christ to summarize his mission on earth, to live life to the fullest is to dwell in the satisfaction that can only be derived from consistently helping others to thrive despite the inconvenience to us. It is the unabashed willingness to assume the daunting positions that were left vacant by the weak, irresponsible, fearful, prideful, ignorant, greedy, arrogant and wicked, and to do this despite obstructions, oppositions and oppressions. Be you a spouse, parent, child, or in any form of leadership, to live life to the fullest means to do more than is expected of you and to give much more than you have ever received without dwelling on the imbalance. It is to be readily available to make a sacrificial difference in the lives of others without waiting to be asked. It is to inspire, to motivate, to encourage, to exhort and to be a blessing to others regardless of the challenges of your own situation.

Those who live their lives to the fullest love despite excruciating hate, persevere despite severe challenges, maintain integrity despite overwhelming adversity, appreciate despite abounding lack and encourage despite aggressive opposition. While the acts of self-actualization may be visible to others, the acts of living life to the fullest are often unannounced, often anonymous. The main difference between self-actualization and living life to the fullest is the true motive behind each act of sacrifice involved, which can only be measured by you and God. The one week you spent in that leprosy camp may only be an act of self-actualization if not done with a pure motive and out of unconditional love. It is one thing to be an achiever in the eyes of men, and quite another to be an achiever in the eyes of God. The latter is living life to the fullest.

For many years, I chose to believe that fulfillment was measured by wealth and health, by network and net worth. I chose to believe that living life to the fullest literally meant to be ahead of everyone else; to win against other people in everything and to feel good about it. I chose to believe that it meant to stand out, to be recognized and rewarded for whatever contribution I made towards anything, regardless of how minute it may have been. And except you have gone far into your journey en route to fulfillment, your belief about what it means to live life to the fullest may not be too far from this limited thinking as well.

Many of us may agree that living life to the fullest has nothing to do with wealth accumulation; however, if we were to think about what we spend most of our days trying to accomplish, it is most likely to accumulate wealth rather than to distribute love. It is most likely to secure our comfort rather than to provide others with comfort. To live life to the fullest is to be in a heightened level of physical, mental and emotional being that can only be understood when viewed from a spiritual perspective. It is about being absolutely content, with or without riches. It is about making sacrifices for the betterment of others, regardless of the cost to us.

If you are familiar with the biblical story of a widow who donated her only coin in the temple while others who gave more than she did only gave a fraction of their riches, then behold an example of someone who lived life to the fullest. In the words of Mahatma Ghandi, "The sacrifice which causes sorrow to the doer of the sacrifice is no sacrifice. Real sacrifice lightens the mind of the doer and gives him a sense of peace and joy." To live life to the fullest, we would have arrived at a point in our journey en route to fulfillment where we consider it pure joy to be sacrificial, where our gentleness is evident to all; where fear is inexistence, worry is foreign, and pain is training.

At this stage in our journey en route to fulfillment, what we do is no longer as important as the heart with which it is done; it is no longer as important as the impact of what we do. For it is the motive and impact of what we do that would determine how well what we do is perceived by God. As Apostle Paul puts it, "Whatever you do, whether in word or deed, do it all in the name of the Lord Jesus, giving thanks to God the Father through him." This is the stage in the journey where some people unfortunately quit the marathon of life because of pressure from their egos. It is also the stage where the determined are exposed to a whole new way of being, where the open are elevated to a whole new level of thinking, which is almost irreversible.

A good example is the biblical story of the rich young ruler who came to Jesus wanting to know what it means to live life to the fullest. As the story goes, this rich young ruler had been able to impressively amass wealth without having broken any of the Ten Commandments. But when Jesus Christ asked him to sell all his possession and give to the poor, "he went away sad, because he had great wealth". Based on the lives of those who have moved from self-actualization to self-fulfillment, I have learnt that everyone has a daily quota of love to contribute towards filling the lives of others, towards making the world a better place; an expectation that we must all strive to meet, an expectation that we will be measured against either in this life or in the life to come.

Inasmuch as it is wise to save money for the future, it is unwise to give up opportunities of impacting others because of the need to save for a future that we are not even guaranteed of. Living life to the fullest is as near the end of the journey en route to fulfillment as possible in a lifetime. Wealth is great, but of what use is it if it stands to benefit only the wealthy. It is like having the cure for cancer and sharing it with only those who have no cancer. Whether you are rich or not, you are not if your richness is benefitting no one else but yourself. Why seek to be appreciated by men when your ultimate destination is determined by God? If there was ever a time to sacrifice everything we have to build a legacy that would determine where we stand before God, it is now.

Whether we see it like that or not, our life is not for us to keep, but rather for us to give. It is not for us to hoard, but rather for us to share. It is not for us to save but rather, for us to expend. These are the imperatives of a fulfilled life; what it means to live life to the fullest. Those who cling unto their lives with both hands would never be able to see how beautiful it really is. It may have been about us in the beginning of this journey, but from this point onwards, it is now about enabling the journey of others, about building a legacy that would last forever. Why even bother reaching the peak of the mountain if you will eventually die there alone?

Besides the obvious deterrents of fulfillment like pride, laziness, selfishness and greed, the most common subtler traits that deter people from living their lives to the fullest are fear, guilt, shame, self-pity and timidity. In my case, it was guilt; guilt from the unscrupulous activities that I had engaged in during my days of rebellion. My arrogance had hurt many, my greed had caused me to defraud others, and my pride had inflicted pain on others. And when I am not alert enough, this guilt will proceed to create self-pity in me, making me to feel unworthy about living life to the fullest.

If I harbour the thought for too long, I will begin to question myself and purpose in life. If I don't take this negative thought captive at this point, self-pity will give birth to shame, through flashbacks of the lies I told in my days of rebellion, and the countless people I deceived, defrauded, defamed and disappointed. While whether we forgive or are forgiving does not necessarily erase the past, forgiveness is meant to change the bitterness of our past into a hope for our future. It is meant to create opportunities to be humble and contrite, loving and lovable. It is one thing to be forgiven by God, another thing to be forgiven by others, and quite another to forgive ourselves.

Some people may wonder who are we to exhort others to greater heights when we committed many atrocities in the past. They may wonder who are we to teach others about what it means to live life to the fullest when we derailed many people from their journey en route to fulfillment during our days of rebellion. We may have discovered ourselves, become self-aware, and even now, actualizing our dreams, but who are we to challenge anyone about integrity, humility and authenticity when we may have lacked them for the most part of our lives? When I compare my previous way of being to my new way of being, I can only consider myself very honoured by God to have been given a second chance to redeem myself and dwell in His Grace.

Who are we not to exhort others to greater heights if, despite our past atrocities, we are now blazing our own trails to fulfillment? Who are we not to challenge others about integrity, humility and authenticity when, despite having lacked them for the most part of our lives, we are now making every effort to embody them for the rest of our lives? Who are we not to teach others about what it means to live life to the fullest when, despite having derailed so many people in the past from their journey, we are now passionately enabling even more people to remain on the narrow road. We may not be able to turn back the hands of time, but we can ensure that the time we have left in this world is wisely spent to make it a better place than it was when we first came into it.

To live life to the fullest, we must cross over from just renouncing our atrocities to courageously announcing our beliefs. We must cross over from just confessing our sins to soundly professing our faith. After having come this far in my journey, grateful for the support of those who helped me work through the challenges of self-discovery, self-awareness and self-actualization, I have learnt that humility is more important than rightness. If I have hurt you, may God bring you comfort. If I have caused you pain, may God strengthen you. If I have defrauded you, may God reward you tenfold. In our journey en route to fulfillment, apologies may have to be tendered and repercussions may have to be faced, but those who wish to live life to the fullest will determinedly confront them all.

What a relief it is to rid ourselves of whatever is weighing down our hearts, hindering our progress, and troubling our souls. In the words of Apostle Paul, "I thank Christ Jesus our Lord, who has given me strength, that he considered me trustworthy, appointing me to his service. Even though I was once a blasphemer and a persecutor and a violent man, I was shown mercy because I acted in ignorance and unbelief. The grace of our Lord was poured out on me abundantly, along with the faith and love that are in Christ Jesus. Here is a trustworthy saying that deserves full acceptance: Christ Jesus came into the world to save sinners–of whom I am the worst. But for that very reason I was shown mercy so that in me, the worst of sinners, Christ Jesus might display his immense patience as an example for those who would believe in him and receive eternal life. Now to the King eternal, immortal, invisible, the only God, be honour and glory for ever and ever. Amen". I could not have said this any better.

Our past way of being is not an excuse for not beginning our journey en route to fulfillment. Our current way of being is not an excuse for not wanting to live life to the fullest. Where we are in life is not an excuse for not being where we should be by now. Even though they may be deterrents of fulfillment, fear, guilt, shame, self-pity and timidity are never to blame for not choosing to live our lives to the fullest. It is only when we accept full responsibility for our action and inaction that we can begin the process of welcoming greatness into our lives. Until then, the chasm between us and greatness will continue to widen. We have to be very careful to ensure that whatever we claim to be holding us back from living our lives to the fullest are not disguised schemes of our egos, subtle ploys of the devil.

My greatest sin then was to think so highly of myself because of the successes of my schemes. My greatest sin then was to congratulate myself for fame and riches that were accomplished at the demise of others. What a pitiable state to be; to be applauded by the world and yet despised by heaven. In the words of Prophet Amos, "The swift will not escape, the strong will not muster their strength, and the warrior will not save his life." My greatest joy now is to know that God thinks highly of me. It is to know that I am valued, not necessarily in the eyes of the world, but in the heart of heaven. I feel so honoured to be involved in the lives of many, to be entrusted with responsibilities which I had previously thought were only meant for people like Abraham Lincoln, Martin Luther King Jr., Nelson Mandela and Mother Teresa. My greatest joy now is to know that regardless of where we are in life or the excuses we make for not living our lives to the full, we were all born as equals and regarded by God as equals.

Poise and serenity are amongst the qualities that make angels fly. When we are calm, careful, calculated and compassionate in our endeavours, making every effort to not allow our ungodly past, the ungodly behaviours of others, and unfavourable conditions of our environment overshadow the image and likeness of God in us, we would become poised enough to soar, serene enough to walk on water, and confident enough to move mountains. We will become comfortable enough to speak without shame, courageous enough to act without fear, and compassionate enough to work without prejudice. We will begin to live life to the fullest, and, like Apostle Paul, would have succeeded in "fighting the good fight, finishing the race, and keeping the faith".

According to King Solomon, "Of making many books there is no end and much study wearies the body. Now all has been heard; here is the conclusion of the matter: Fear God and keep his commandments; this is the duty of all mankind. For God will bring every deed into judgment, including every hidden thing, whether it is good or evil." Just as a baby is in grave danger without the mother or someone else to care for him, so is a branch destined to wither if severed from its tree, so is man vulnerable to pain and susceptible to evil without God.

Welcome to Greatness!

Almighty God,

To live life to the fullest is a gift from you! To even begin to understand what that means requires your gift of discernment! What an amazing concept! What an amazing opportunity!!

Thank you, Lord, for giving us the chance to know you, to heed your call to move from self-actualization to self-fulfillment. Thank you, Lord, for creating the world in such a way that there is always something we can do for another. Thank you, Lord, that we have the capability and capacity to be a blessing to someone else, to know your will for us.

As I conclude this book, I ask, Lord, that every word of wisdom gained from it resides in my heart and mind forever! May the end of this book be the beginning of a whole new journey for me; a journey to know you better, to serve others wholeheartedly and to be a representative of love like you have called us to be.

As I conclude this book, Lord, may I be able and willing to share the knowledge therein with those around me. May my life never be the same to the glory of your name. May peace and harmony, love and compassion, and grace and kindness rest and abide with me now and forever.

Like Prophet Isaiah, Lord, here am I, send me to bring healing to the hurting, peace to the troubled, love to the loveless, and compassion to the confused.

Thank you, Lord, for listening to my prayers, for granting me your heart desires for me.

Amen

Afterword

The mother of Zebedee's sons came to Jesus with her sons and, kneeling down, asked a favour of him.

"What is it you want?" he asked.

She said, "Grant that one of these two sons of mine may sit at your right and the other at your left in your kingdom."

"You don't know what you are asking," Jesus said to them. "Can you drink the cup I am going to drink?"

"We can," they answered.

Jesus said to them, "You will indeed drink from my cup, but to sit at my right or left is not for me to grant. These places belong to those for whom they have been prepared by my Father."

When the ten heard about this, they were indignant with the two brothers. Jesus called them together and said, "You know that the rulers of the Gentiles lord it over them, and their high officials exercise authority over them. Not so with you. Instead, whoever wants to become great among you must be your servant, and whoever wants to be first must be your slave–just as the Son of Man did not come to be served, but to serve, and to give his life as a ransom for many."

By Apostle Matthew
Disciple of Jesus Christ

Acknowledgement

Since the inception of this book, God has blessed me through many people; people who deserve the credit for this book way more than I do. Many of them have taught me things that changed my life for the better, while many more have allowed me to become part of their lives through coaching and mentorship. But first and foremost though, I thank Almighty God for making it happen in ways that could only be divine.

Rich Worthington, a true coach and mentor who taught me so much about life, leadership and love. Rich, I learnt a lot from you even in instances when you did not open your mouth. Your exemplary devotion to God, service to humanity, and Christ-like attitude will be remembered for generations to come.

Samina Deen, a true friend in everyway. Samina, I thank you for always stepping up to whatever needed to be done to make this dream a reality. May God continue to honour you for your openness, humility and love.

Jason Monaco, a true friend and business associate. Your absolute confidence in me and in the impact of this book, coupled with your honourable desire to embody the principle it promotes, humbles me. With a beautiful heart like yours, your better days are obviously ahead of you.

Ann Franklin, your unabashed belief in me was instrumental in both my journey en route to fulfillment and in the writing of this book. Your diligence, dedication and devotion to this book is worthy of praise. I always looked forward to the encouraging words that you consistently embedded in your responses. That is so angelic of you!

Nadene Joachim, a woman of noble character, for the nights you gave up to edit contents upon contents, even while you were pregnant! Truly, Nadene, you are a woman of noble character and it is only God who can repay your kind-heartedness and remarkable effort in this book.

It would be remiss on my part to not mention how deeply indebted I am to my children for their patience with me throughout the writing of this book. For the food, fellowship and fun times that I skipped to meet crucial timelines, I apologize to you, Brandie, Travis, Naomi and Luc. Regardless of the mistakes of your parents, may each one of you grow up to become embodiment of greatness and epitome of love. There is no person or thing that would be able to hinder my love and appreciation for you.

Special thanks to my parents, Anthony and Mary Ogbeide-Ihama, and my siblings, Don Ogbeide-Ihama and Faith Iwu, whose belief in me I pray other people are able to experience with their family as well. Thank you for allowing God to use you to lead me through the experiences I had to go through in order to become who I was created to be. Thank you for your consistent sacrifices and support, for your continuous love and prayers, for the unity we share in the family.

About the Author

For many years, Alex Ihama has been redefining greatness for varieties of audiences across the world–Organization Leaders, Business Executives, Entrepreneurs, Politicians, Professional Athletes, Community and Religious Leaders, University and High School Students, and diverse and unique groups of men, women and youths.

An Author and a Life, Business and Executive Coach, Alex is considered by many to be one of the most passionate keynote speakers of his era. He is often sought-after for his extensive knowledge and experiences which he claims to have acquired from his very graphic childhood, his deep researches on life, spiritual and business matters, his wide intercontinental travels, the numerous leadership positions he held in reputable organizations, his constant interactions with sages and gurus, and his consistent involvement in literally thousands of lives all over the world through events, coaching, and the countless community activities he regularly participates in.

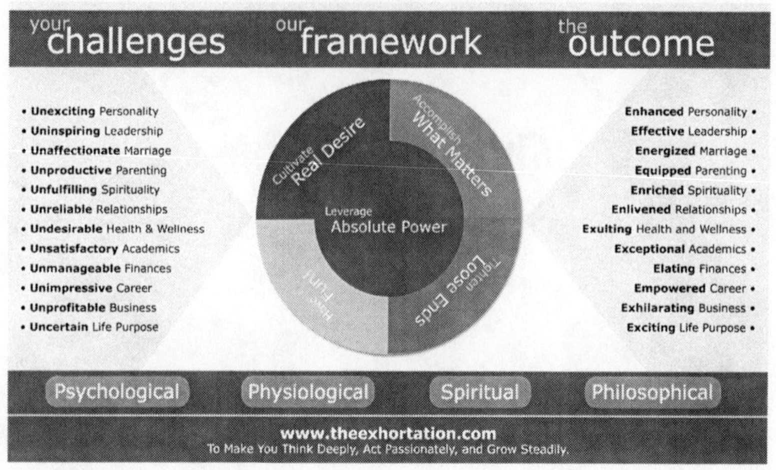

Regardless of the industry or profession, Alex delivers "passionate messages that stick" at Leadership Conferences, Sales Conventions, Religious Places, Non-Profit Organizations, High School and University Ceremonies, and other events that are organized to "Exhort People to Greatness in Life, Leadership and Love".

According to Alex, "I was born to do this and could do nothing else better than travelling far and wide to passionately introduce people to the gems within themselves, to share the knowledge and encouragement people need to become their best selves, to help people become what they were created to be, to help others welcome greatness into their lives and businesses. I will forever be in the hot pursuit of the knowledge that is necessary for me to teach others what may be holding them back from the peace of mind that they so desperately seek. My life purpose is clear; it is very clear to me and to those who I am fortunate to know. I was born 'To make people think deeply, act passionately and grow steadily'. This . . . I will do all the days of my life".

Alex's messages are based on deep psychological, physiological, spiritual and philosophical researches, which transcend religious, cultural, racial and socio-economic backgrounds. His messages are very thought-provoking, remarkably intriguing and, according to participants at his events, leaves you in awe of yourself.

CPSIA information can be obtained at www.ICGtesting.com
Printed in the USA
LVOW080158240412

278812LV00001B/6/P